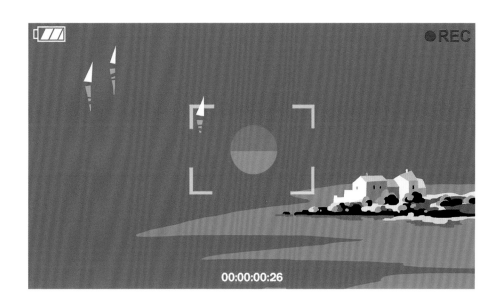

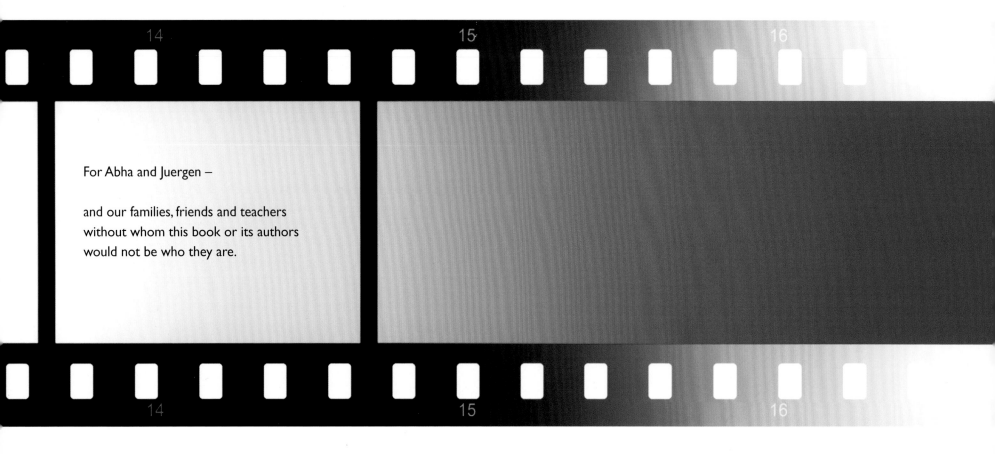

For Abha and Juergen –

and our families, friends and teachers
without whom this book or its authors
would not be who they are.

**A TALISMAN BOOK** FOR LAURENCE KING PUBLISHING

First published in 2018
Second Impression 2019
Third Impression 2021
Fourth Impression 2022
Fifth Impression 2023

Talisman Publishing Pte Ltd
talisman@apdsing.com
www.talismanpublishing.com

All Illustrations © Hans P Bacher
Texts © Hans P Bacher and Sanatan
Suryavanshi
Hans P Bacher has asserted his right
under Copyright, Designs, and Patents
Act 1988 to be identified as the Author
of this Work.

A catalogue record for this book is
available from the British Library.

ISBN 978-1-78627-220-1

Printed in Singapore

# Hans P Bacher

## Color and Composition for Film

## Sanatan Suryavanshi

LAURENCE KING

# contents

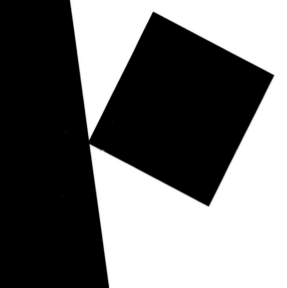

# FOREWORD

Hans Bacher has long established his reputation as one of the great designers of our time in both print and film. His production designs have established the look of seminal animated films at the Walt Disney Studios and Steven Spielberg's Amblin Entertainment. *The Lion King*, *Balto*, *Mulan*, and *Beauty and the Beast* have all relied heavily on his visual style and design work, and his books and blog posts are required reading for millions of fans and students of animation who seek him out.

Like Mary Blair a generation before, Bacher deeply understands the use of color and composition to solicit an emotional response from the audience. His work is bold and unconventional but always grounded in storytelling which makes it invaluable for the study of film, illustration, story-boarding, and cinematography. *Vision — Color and Composition for Film* represents this artist's amazing depth of knowledge, all shared with clarity and striking visual examples that open up new worlds of understanding to Bacher's incredible craft.

Don Hahn
Executive Producer
*The Lion King, Maleficent,
Beauty and the Beast*

This is not a book about technique. It's not going to teach you how to speedpaint in Photoshop, control the exposure on a Canon camera or previz a sequence using Maya. These are important things to know, depending on your medium, but you probably already have books on your shelf that can help with them.

This book, instead, attempts to teach you something more foundational. Something that applies across mediums and actually defines the goal you subsequently use all those techniques to achieve: *Seeing* and *thinking* like a visual storyteller. Books are read, songs heard and films watched. Cinema is first and foremost a visual art form and relies, primarily, on imagery to tell its stories.

'A Film is never really good unless the Camera is an Eye in the head of a Poet'
Orson Welles

# Introduction

Therefore, how effective we are in telling these stories depends on how well we understand this visual language and communicate within it.

Images, like most things, have an underlying science defining how they work. This science can be studied, understood, and then used to get consistently successful results. In the following pages, we will attempt to demystify that science and talk through it in bite-sized chunks you can process. The format of this book has been designed with this idea of bite-sized chunks in mind. Individual chapters have been kept as brief as possible and designed to stand alone. You can progress through in a linear fashion, or start with the first few chapters and then jump around to an order you prefer. Visual artists tend to be visual learners. Keeping this in mind, we've tried our best to show rather than tell and designed the pages in a way that hopefully inspires as much as informs.

Even though both the authors have a background in animation, we believe the concepts discussed here are applicable to a wide variety of fields. We have tried our best to keep away from industry specific terms and kept the conversation at a level that can be understood by a beginner with no former knowledge of the subject.

Learning composition and color is a lifelong journey. As exciting as it is challenging. We hope that these pages can help you find your feet on this road and perhaps even deepen your ability to enjoy the view. Let's get started.

# THE VISUAL COMMUNICATION PROCESS

Films and television use thousands of images stitched together to tell a story. Understanding how each of these impacts us individually brings us closer to controlling how they impact us as a whole. So, what actually happens in your head when you look at an image?

# Several things. And all in a split second!

To begin with, your mind tries to make sense of it all. Shapes, colors, lines, etc. are all processed by your brain. So, it can conclude if it is looking at a face, a person, a house, or all of the above.

Once all the main ingredients have been identified, your brain puts this information in context with all the other things it knows. So, for instance, if the shot is of the Eiffel tower, it will assume you are in Paris. This is a simple example, but the mind constantly makes all sorts of deductions from the images you are seeing. Simultaneously it will take into consideration what you saw in the previous shot as well as something you might remember from years ago.

Thirdly, the image will evoke certain emotions. Often before you can even understand what you are looking at! Images can make you feel a sense of joy, dread, fear or excitement, without you knowing why you are feeling those things. Sometimes, this is because of the design choices, such as color combinations or rhythm used in the composition, and, other times, it might be because you associate something you see on the screen with something from your past.

All of these things happen simultaneously and almost automatically. This automatic processing is where the seemingly magical power that images have to control us comes from. And it is what we are going to explore in this book.

We will look at how each element of design relates to these automatic processes and explore how that can be used to your advantage. We will change our mindset from someone who just consumes images to someone who studies them. We will look at things more deeply and mine each visual, until we can identify what are the tools it is employing.

If you have the tools to break down everything you see to its basic visual building blocks, you can learn from everything. If you can understand why these blocks make you feel the way they do, you can use that knowledge to recreate that feeling in your audience. Making these fundamental building blocks accessible when you see is key to developing your visual aesthetic. This is the goal for which the subsequent chapters have been designed.

WHY DO CERTAIN PICTURES MAKE US FEEL RELAXED WHILE OTHERS SCARE US

# THE PSYCHOLOGY OF IMAGES

WHY ARE CERTAIN COLOR COMBINATIONS EXCITING AND OTHERS DEPRESSING

BEFORE WE LEARN HOW TO USE IMAGES TO MANIPULATE EMOTIONS WE NEED TO UNDERSTAND WHY IMAGES AFFECT US IN THE FIRST PLACE

# ASSOCIATION

Think of a time you were relaxing at the beach. Do you remember hearing the sounds of seagulls squawking, children playing and waves lapping the shore? Do you remember noticing the bright beach towels, warm sunlit sand and crystal blue water? What kind of emotions does thinking of the beach evoke? How different is this from what you remember seeing and feeling that one time you hurried down a dark alley?

Our lives are made up of millions of evocative experiences. Memories of beach trips, walking down dark alleys, or curling up on a favorite couch with a cup of cocoa and a book all feed into your brain for future reference. These memories consist of a lot of things: an unusual color combination you noticed, a typical sound you heard, a particular smell in the air or taste in your mouth. The key is you also felt a particular way while experiencing these.

Over time, subconsciously your brain starts to link these elements with the emotion that surrounds them.

Warm sand and a cool ocean become synonymous with relaxation; back alleys and dark ambiguous shapes evoke fear and suspicion. Today, even the experience of watching movies has created pools of associations of their own. A beautiful girl in a red dress, a half-lit figure standing in the corner of a dark room, a seedy neon sign displaying 'MOTEL', to use a few cinema tropes, all evoke distinct and powerful expectations in the audience generated by memories of similar movie moments they have watched.

As a visual storyteller, you need to be aware of all the associations you are tapping into through your choice of shape, color, light and motif in an image. What memory is each of these evoking? What moods are those connected to? Is this mood appropriate to your scene? Should any of these elements be replaced with something more evocative? Taking the time to curate the right elements and cue appropriate associations when constructing an image will dramatically increase the impact on your audience.

WE SEE, SOUNDS WE HEAR, FOOD WE TASTE. EMOTIONAL STATES THAT SURROUND THEM.

# MECHANICS

There is an underlying dynamic at work in every image created purely by the interplay of visual elements in the frame. This occurs on an abstract level, independent of what these shapes and colors represent.

Red and green placed next to each other, for instance, generate contrast and excitement. This holds true whether it is a red car in a green warehouse or a red dress in a green room. Similarly, some shapes tend to work together and others against each other, some lines are harmonious and others contrasting. Different kinds of interactions, such as visual symmetry or asymmetry, harmony or contrast, balance or imbalance, create very different kinds of visual energy.

Rooted heavily in an understanding of fundamental design principles, learning to see these abstract underlying picture 'mechanics' is essential to creating effective compositions for film. We will delve deeper into how these mechanics can be used in the later chapters, but for now start making an effort to look past what the objects in a composition represent and focus more on what's happening between the shapes, lines and colors they are made of.

The great abstractionists often use nothing but the interaction of visual elements to generate an emotional impact in their paintings. Imagine how powerful an image that combines this with the right motif can be. Once you learn to 'see' these mechanics at play, you start to notice that they are the backbone of the world's best cinematography.

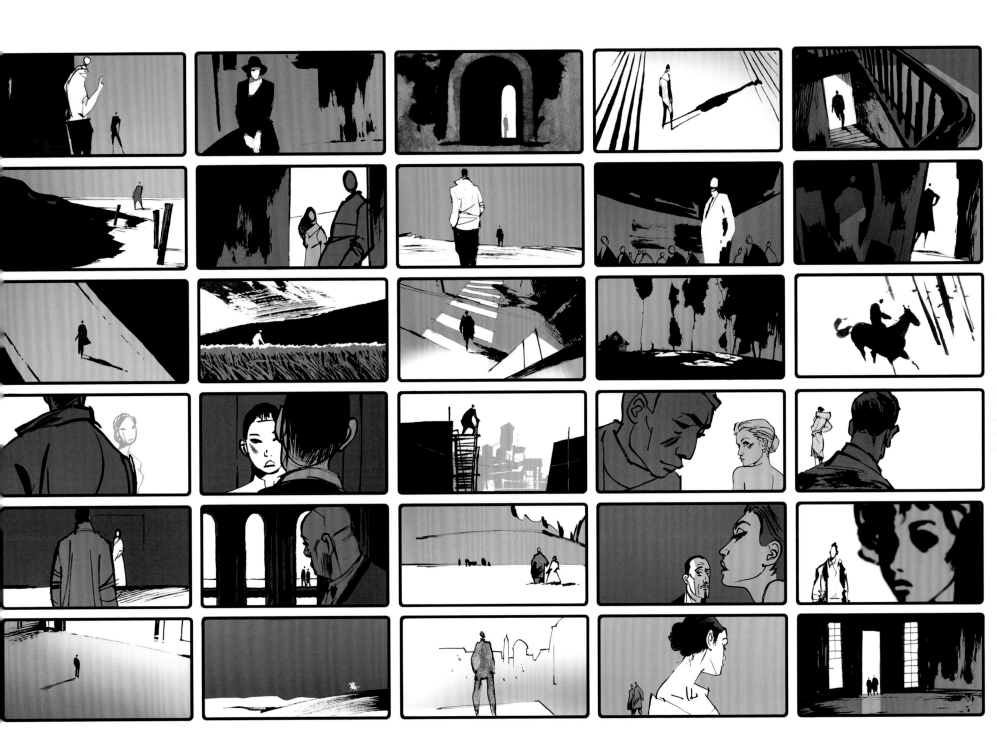

# RESONANCE IS WHAT HAPPENS WHEN YOU ALIGN WHAT YOU ARE SAYING WITH HOW YOU ARE SAYING IT

# RESONANCE

Imagine a sign which says 'NO TRESPASSING!' written in baby pink, flowery, cursive handwriting on a light yellow board. How much of an impact do you think this warning would have on you? Now imagine the same words written in capital letters with a thick, red, bold, no-nonsense military font on a black metal sign. Carries a different ring to it, doesn't it? This is an example of resonance.

Resonance is what happens when you align *what* you are saying with *how* you are saying it. This, fundamentally, is what powerful visual communication is all about. Long ago, visual artists discovered that relating the nature and content of a message to the visual elements involved in communicating it dramatically increases its effectiveness. The two signs saying 'Keep Out' are both communicating the same basic information, but the more effective of the two is the one saying it literally and visually. Good visual storytelling is no different.

Lines, shapes, colors, lights, camera angles, staging, choreography and design are all part of the grammar that composes the language of visual storytelling. These are the elements we manipulate to visually translate what the script needs us to communicate. A line in the script such as 'John was shot' can be visualized in 100 different ways. Each choice you make regarding where you place the camera, how big John is on the screen, time of day, lighting setup and so on all contribute to how the audience feels about John being shot. Getting the right blend of visuals to showcase the scripted event will increase the effectiveness of the shot tenfold.

Making a shot resonate requires a thorough understanding of two things: 'speaking' fluently using the elements of design; and identifying the right emotion for a given shot. These are elaborated upon in some of the later chapters.

As your understanding of each design element grows, always attempt to use it in combination with the story requirements of the shot. Every little decision will affect your frame. Ultimately no color choice, camera placement, or design decision of any sort should be random or accidental. Simply put, the right blend of form and content invariably makes for the most compelling film frames. Mastery of this art will allow you to design compelling shots that stay with your audience long after they have left the theater.

GO

Stop

icecold

hot

LOVE STORY

Keep these ideas of association, picture mechanics and resonance at the back of your mind as you go through the book. Analyze every image in it as well as around you. Always try to understand on the most basic level why something you see makes you feel the way it does. What visual elements may be contributing to that feeling? What associations or primal instincts could this visual be trying to target? What memories could the choice of light and color be tapping into?

What of the picture mechanics? How are the fundamental design elements playing against each other in the frame? Is the image chaotic? Is it organised? And are all of these things aligned with what the subject matter of the image is? Is it resonating? Are there ways that it could be made to resonate more?

Asking yourself questions like these will deepen your awareness of how your mind is processing an image. This in turn will help you understand how your images will process in the minds of an audience. This is the basis for building an understanding of visual language.

There is no one 'correct' way to communicate visually, any more than there is only one way to communicate using words. Ultimately, over time, you will develop your own style and unique approach. In a way, your own 'voice'. It is this unique approach, specific to you, that is ultimately of greatest value.

However, if you stay constantly engaged in soaking up and analyzing images around you, you will get there a lot faster.

# THE ANATOMY OF AN IMAGE

There are several dimensions to any image. In order for us to analyze a particular visual and discuss the mechanisms that make it work, you need to be familiar with what these are. In the illustration on right and overleaf, the different aspects of an image are identified. Many of these areas are covered in individual chapters in the book, and all of them are dealt with in greater detail later on. For now, it is important for you to have a working knowledge of what each term means.

The next double page should be photocopied and kept where you work. Refer to it constantly until it is internalized. Whenever you have a few minutes to spare, try taking an image and dissecting it into the different parts shown in these pages. You will notice immediately that you start looking at things a lot more deeply and see interesting possibilities that previously you may have missed. Maybe an object next to your desk is uninteresting at first glance, but has an interesting silhouette? Soon you will be constantly milking the visual world around you for potential raw materials, and learning to see beauty in everything. This way of 'looking' is the first step in your visual education. On top of that, you will never get bored while waiting for the bus again.

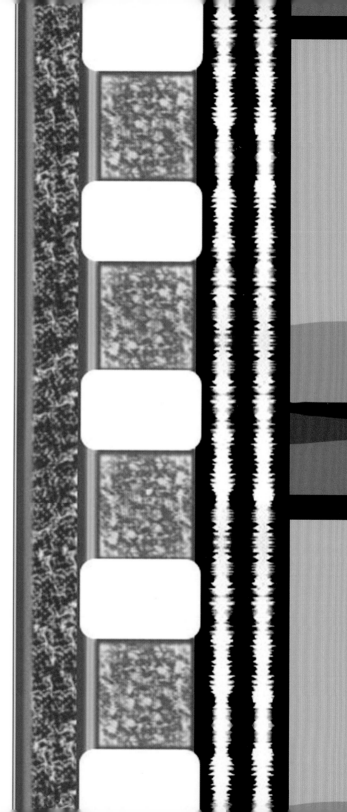

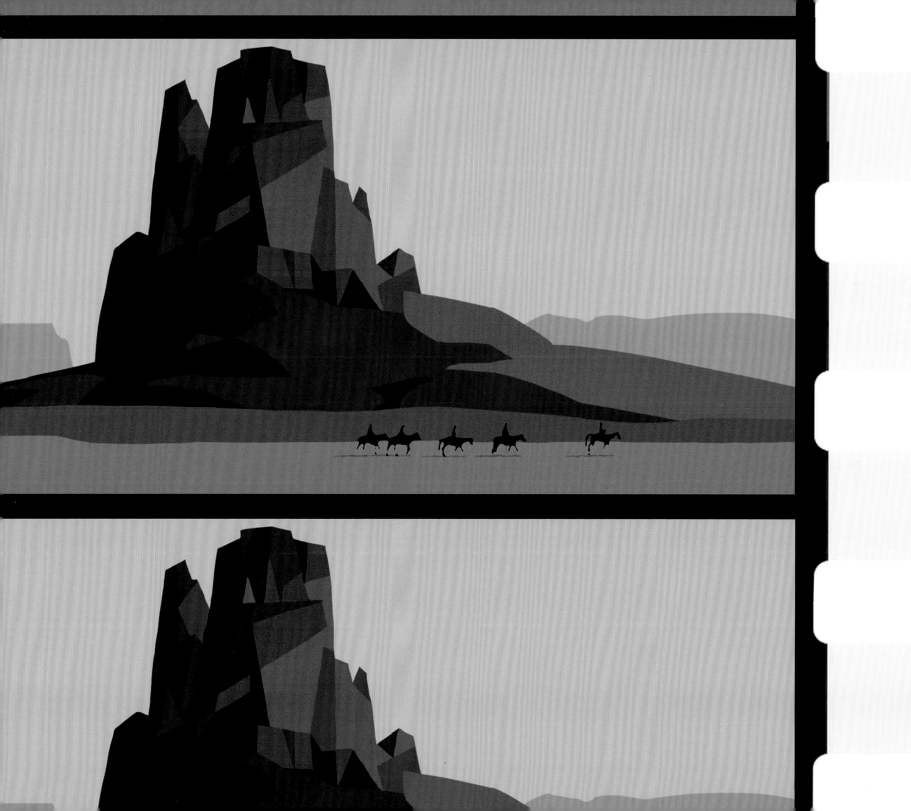

**Subject** — The main motif or focus. Your choice of subject says a lot to the viewer. You may be framing a rose, but focusing on the thorns as opposed to the petals sends out very different signals.

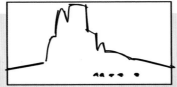

**Format** — The shape and proportion of the length and breadth of an image. Different formats complement different kinds of shots and storytelling.

3:4

superwide

**Orientation** — More an illustration term than a film one, this refers to the horizontal or vertical aspect of your format. Tailor this to suit your subject. For example, traditional portraits work better oriented vertically, whereas landscapes are usually horizontal.

poster

**Framing** — How your subject sits within your composition. Is it tiny in the frame or filling it? Does it show the entire subject or crop it in an intriguing way? Is it placed near the top of the frame or right at the bottom?

**Line** — The linear component. All compositions contain visible as well as invisible lines. The dominant direction of these goes a long way in affecting the energy in the scene.

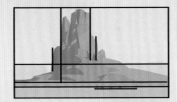

positive shape

negative shape

**Shape** — The major divisions of space within the frame. All well thought through compositions are made up of a small number of major positive as well as negative shapes. Learn to see the big shapes in a composition.

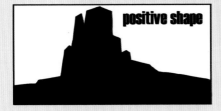

lights

midtones

darks

**Value** — The degree of lightness or darkness. This greyscale version of a composition is the most significant building block for defining color and focal points. Learn to simplify the infinite variations of values in an image into lights, darks and mid-tones.

# ANATOMY IN IMAGE

**Color** — One of the most evocative components of a composition, color is probably the most immediate component. Learn to simplify a composition down to three to five major colors.

**Pattern** — An overall design or repeated element which holds the composition together. Pattern can be used to unify a composition that contains a lot of disparate elements.

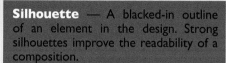

**Silhouette** — A blacked-in outline of an element in the design. Strong silhouettes improve the readability of a composition.

**Texture** — Indication of the tactile quality of a component. Texture can be used to indicate nearness, fight flatness and balance the composition. It must be used with great restraint.

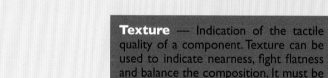

**Light** — The illuminating element. Light is the designing factor for several of the other aspects of the image. Observe the source, intensity and quality.

**Depth** — The relative flatness or sense of space in a picture. It can be controlled by depth of field as well as relaxing or forcing perspective.

**Edge** — The quality of the separations between the shapes. The predominance of soft versus hard edges can greatly alter the feel of a composition.

**Movement** — Any moving element. A major consideration when composing for film, this has to be as carefully positioned and choreographed as any other element of the composition.

# LINE
## COMING UP

It might be tempting to skip over something seemingly so elementary, but don't be fooled by its simple appearance. There are many dimensions to good compositional lines and many ways they can add drama to the frame. Used masterfully, lines by themselves can be confident or nervous, graceful or chaotic, stiff or organic. Understanding relationships between different lines in an image can be used to make the same basic content feel dangerous or calm, serious or playful. You need to become aware of various aspects that define the power of lines and understand how to use them to your advantage. But before you can learn to control lines, you must learn to see them.

Let us begin with the most basic element of design — the line. In film, this refers to 'compositional lines' that connect two or more things in a frame, providing a path for the eye to travel on. The types of lines used in a composition, and how they relate to each other, affect how quickly the audience gets to what they are supposed to see and the emotion the frame evokes along the way.

# LINE

The world is full of lines. When you start paying attention, you'll notice them everywhere. A lot of these are probably contributing right now to how the 'scene' feels wherever you may be sitting and reading this book. Developing an increased sensitivity to this in real life, as well as in film, is a necessary first step towards training your eye. Equally essential, however, is learning to separate the lines that matter from the ones that don't.

# STRUCTURAL LINES

Each shot has a few basic structural lines that form the core skeleton of a composition. Some are obvious, like the edges of a dominant tonal shape; others are felt rather than seen, like the mental connections we draw between characters looking at each other. Learning to see these structural lines is the first step towards understanding how to use line in shot composition. The images on this page illustrate some examples of where lines are found in film frames.

Four structural lines every shot contains are made by the borders of your frame. Being mindful of these as you design your composition simply cannot be overstated. (1–12)

Figures in a composition create structural lines through their orientation. (1–9)

The tilt of a character's head or lean of its body creates structural lines in close ups and medium shots. (9, 12)

The edges of dominant tonal masses create structural lines. (2, 3)

The perspective of a shot creates structural lines through repeating elements and diminishing shapes.(4, 7)

Our perception creates structural lines by giving closure to 'broken' shapes. (7, 11)

Certain objects make distinct lines in the composition because of actual or implied movement. (9, 10)

Foreground elements are often used to place additional lines in the frame. (6)

Our perception draws mental lines between major focal points in the frame like these two characters. (5)

Weather effects like rain and snow can make lines through their direction and movement. (9)

Analyze shots, illustrations and your environment using this approach. Where else can you find these lines in a composition? Boil complexity down to its visual essence by identifying the major directions, divisions and movements. Doing such distilled studies will sharpen your perception and sensitize you to the presence and inner dynamics of lines all around you.

Now that you are aware of the variety of structural lines present in a composition, let's consider how we can use this knowledge to generate an emotional impact.

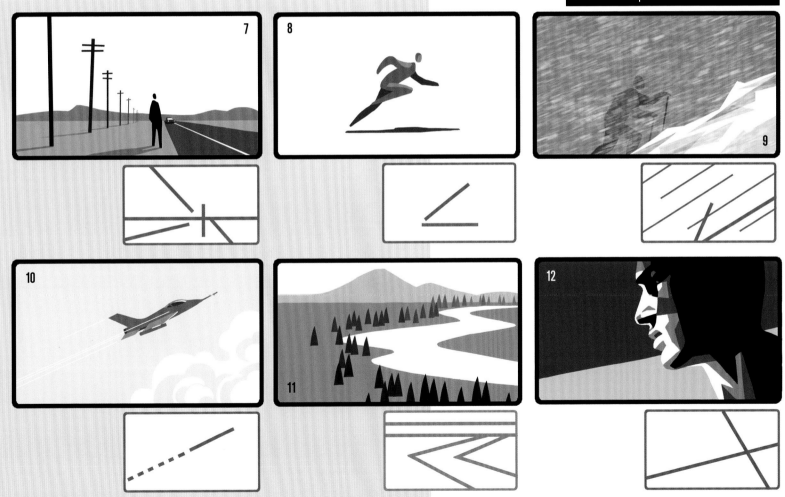

# ORIENTATION

Orientation refers to how a line is positioned with respect to the edge of the frame. Depending on whether the lines in a composition are horizontal, vertical or something in between, the emotional quality of the image will change. A majority of horizontals, for example, tends to give the composition a calm and serene feeling. These lines are in total harmony with the edge of the frame and positioned in the most passive and restful state. Horizontals are often associated with horizons, water bodies and large open spaces. Verticals, on the other hand, stand tall and upright, defying gravity and emphasizing adjectives like strength and elegance. Verticals tend to evoke things which tower over us such as trees and buildings. Diagonals are the most dramatic line orientation you can have in an image. These sharply contrast the horizontals and verticals along the edge of the frame and make for dynamic images which emphasize drama and energy. Diagonals are associated with imbalance and a sense of movement. Orientation can also be used to emphasize a dimension of your frame. Through a dominance of verticals or horizontals, you can shift focus to the length or height of objects in the composition.

Beyond these basic examples, experimenting with line orientation will make you aware of how this can be used to signify a whole host of other emotions, especially when they are combined with the right motif.

To develop a feel for orientation, play with different orientations of a subject in a minimalistic composition. It is important not to get distracted with complexity at this stage. First focus on understanding the basic concept. Just two lines can be enough to begin with. Pay attention to how positioning these in different ways changes the feel of the image.

Studying orientation through a camera is another way to develop sensitivity to this dimension. Take pictures of a few simple objects like a tree or a building while changing its orientation. How does this impact the image? Once you are familiar with the fundamental principles you can compose with other subjects and see how this can be applied to different motifs. Analyze art and the world around you for different examples of orientation. How is this affecting the feel of the visual? Could changing the orientation be used to enhance a particular emotion?

Your frame offers you four lines to work with plus two implied lines.

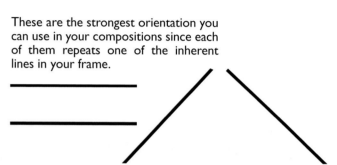

These are the strongest orientation you can use in your compositions since each of them repeats one of the inherent lines in your frame.

Changing the orientation of your subject can change its perceived state.

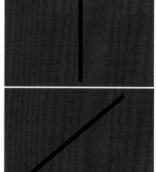

Stable, but still energetic and upright.

Dynamic. Imbalanced and in motion.

Dormant. In a state of rest.

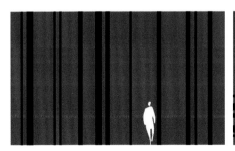

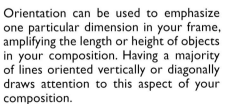

Orientation can be used to emphasize one particular dimension in your frame, amplifying the length or height of objects in your composition. Having a majority of lines oriented vertically or diagonally draws attention to this aspect of your composition.

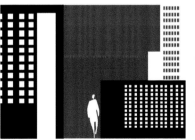

Every location has some essential orientation. Cities and forests generally feel more vertical, while a beach or countryside scene is more horizontal. Dominance in line orientation can be used to amplify some quality of the environment.

Ensure you have a dominant line orientation. Unless you deliberately want a random and chaotic image, pick how the majority of lines in your composition should be oriented based on the informational and emotional requirement of the shot. Minimize all other lines. Having several directions of line in the same strength will cause the composition to be weak, confusing or unspecific.

# PLACEMENT

When designing your composition, pay close attention to how major lines divide space in the frame. The relationship between the resulting shapes has a lot to do with how the composition feels. Symmetrical divisions such as a line cutting through the center of the frame generally make for very static shots. Such perfect divisions are rarely found in nature and do not appeal to our sense of proportion. Asymmetrical space divisions, on the other hand, can vary from being visually interesting to discomforting, depending on whether or not they have balance. Dividing the composition in thirds or using the golden ratio can give examples of balanced asymmetrical space divisions which can be very appealing.

Experiment with different types of space division in your composition. Start by just placing one line within the frame. Now carefully consider the two new spaces created. These shapes can be divided further, symmetrically or asymmetrically. Pay close attention to these new space divisions as you place each subsequent line in your composition. Once you develop sensitivity to this, it will become second nature and you will be able to create appealing compositions with just a handful of lines. Make an analysis of how this concept is used in film frames, interiors and graphic design.

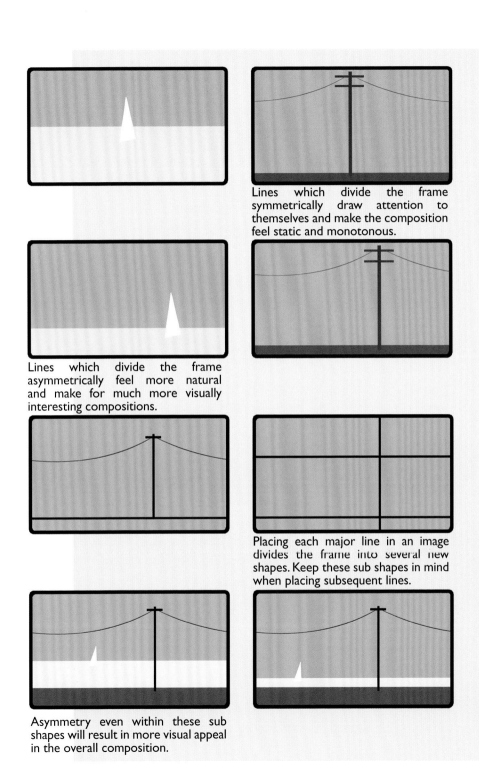

Lines which divide the frame symmetrically draw attention to themselves and make the composition feel static and monotonous.

Lines which divide the frame asymmetrically feel more natural and make for much more visually interesting compositions.

Placing each major line in an image divides the frame into several new shapes. Keep these sub shapes in mind when placing subsequent lines.

Asymmetry even within these sub shapes will result in more visual appeal in the overall composition.

# QUALITY

Lines can zigzag, gently flow, or cut straight across a composition. The quality or nature of lines in your composition is a major evocative component within your image. For example, compositions made strictly with rigid straight lines feel very different from ones composed of gentle curves. Hard straights tend to make for much more graphic visuals which have a certain intensity to them, whereas curved lines usually feel softer and more feminine. There are, of course, infinite variations possible within these. Hard lines can be boring if oriented parallel to the frame and curves can be chaotic if following a random pattern. The goal is to use the nature of lines in an image to emphasize some essential mood or aspect of the environment. For example, a forest scene might have predominantly organic lines amplifying the naturalistic feel in the composition. The interior of a spaceship might instead be full of sleek mechanical lines, giving the image a certain futuristic precision. Be aware of the nature of lines in your image and ensure that they match the subject and mood of the shot.

Each line also has a certain emotional quality due to its thickness. For example, bold lines can make for strong focal points and be used to portray strength or even rigidity. Extremely thin lines, on the other hand, can be suggestive of a certain sophistication and delicacy.

Experiment with different natures of line. It can be a lot of fun just exploring different line types trying to find the right tone for an image. Take some time to walk around your neighborhood photographing the different qualities of line you can find. By developing a sensitivity and awareness to these, you will recognize opportunities for expression all around you.

Analyze the different qualities of line present in your compositions. Can emphasizing any of these be used to further the mood of the composition? Is there a way you can use a particular kind of line to enhance the feel of the visual?

fun...

Combining thick and thin lines can create a lot of rhythm and energy. You can see this at play in drawing. Look at the work of artists like Ronald Searle, Ben Shahn, David Stone Martin and Ralph Steadman. All of their pen and ink drawings are characterized by contrasting line work made up of different thickness, pressure and weight. Try sketching something similar yourself. This playful practice might lead you to discover a new and exciting visual direction that you use in your next project.

Take some time to walk around your neighborhood photographing the different qualities of line you can find. By developing a sensitivity and awareness to these, you will recognize opportunities for expression all around you. Analyze the different qualities of line present in your compositions. Can emphasizing or reducing the importance of any of these be used to further the mood of the composition? Is there a way you could use a particular kind of line to enhance the feel of the visual?

43

Much of the power a line generates in an image is a result of how it works with the other lines in that composition. Depending on how these relate to each other, lines in an image can create rhythm, harmony, disharmony, balance, imbalance and unity. Learning how to generate an emotional impact using multiple lines is essential to designing good compositions.

Bear in mind, even when you start with a blank canvas, you are already working with four lines — the edges of your frame. Every line placed in your composition is therefore already a step towards establishing harmony or contrast within a shot.

Harmonious compositions usually contain lines which are relatively similar in direction and quality. For example, a panoramic view of the ocean with

# HARMONY AND CONTRAST

the horizon parallel to the bottom of the frame would have a lot of repeating harmonious horizontals. Such compositions are great for quieter story moments which require a sense of calm or beauty to prevail in the scene. Too much harmony, however, can be boring and needs to be tempered with contrast and variety. Contrasting compositions often contain energetic lines which follow many different directions. Tilting the same shot of the ocean, for example, would cause tremendous contrast between the diagonals in the image and the edges of the frame. These images are more appropriate for energetic and dramatic story moments requiring greater visual intensity.

Experiment with creating harmony and contrast using a basic compositional setup and try generating different

emotional feels using these. In the beginning, limit yourself to working with only a few lines. This will allow you to focus on how changing the relationships between them affects the composition. Once you are familiar with the basic concept, you can experiment with more complex motifs and see how this principle can be applied. As you go about your day, notice the use of harmony and contrast of lines in the environment around you. Art, architecture and nature are full of examples which can be a constant source of inspiration.

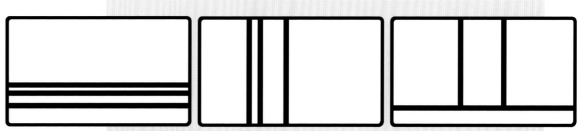

These lines are in harmony with each other and with the borders of the frame.

These lines are in harmony with each other, but in contrast with the frame.

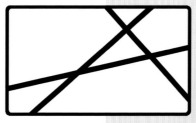  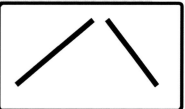

These lines are in contrast with each other and with the frame.

The same is found in curves:

Harmonious

Contrasting

And in a combination of lines and curves:

Harmonious

Contrasting

 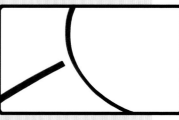

Harmonious lines work together resulting in a minimum of visual tension. These are good choices for shots requiring balance and a sense of calm.

Contrasting lines work against each other and the frame generating a lot of visual tension. These tend to make for imbalanced visuals appropriate for dramatic story moments.

Even non-dramatic compositions can often benefit from some contrast.

Shots containing lines which are in complete harmony with each other can feel flat to the point of being surreal. This is great if it fits the story point, but can otherwise make the composition feel monotonous.

Shots containing lines which have a certain amount of contrast feel much more naturalistic, often providing more visual interest.

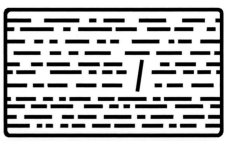

Contrast in lines can also be used to draw attention to a part of the frame.

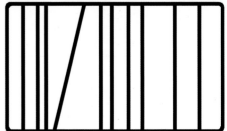

# RHYTHM

Repeating similar lines at certain rhythmic intervals can add another dimension to your composition. Uneven or randomly spaced repetitions tend to add more excitement to the frame and in extreme situations can also add a certain tension. A shattered mirror offers an excellent example of lines following a chaotic rhythm. On the other hand, lines repeating at regular intervals or consistent with a particular proportion can make the composition look organized if used one way and boring if used another. For example, a centrally positioned shot of a church interior would work well with lines made by the pillars repeating at regular intervals. Here the extreme order and organization fits the motif. However, in most shots, such stiff rhythms can look out of place, and create monotony in the composition.

Experiment with creating different emotional impacts using a variety of line rhythms. Start by playing around with a minimalist composition containing only a few lines. Try to find a visual rhythmic equivalent to adjectives like chaotic, dense, serene, elegant, etc.. Once understood, the same principles can be applied to complex shots. Make an analysis of the incredible line rhythms found in nature, art and architecture. Study how the different kinds of rhythm contribute to how they make you feel. The goal is to connect a perception of visual rhythms with an understanding of the emotional impact they create.

Repetition of similar lines creates rhythm in your composition.

Evenly spaced repetitions such as these below create a regular rhythm. This is rarely found in nature and can make a composition look overtly organized and sometimes boring.

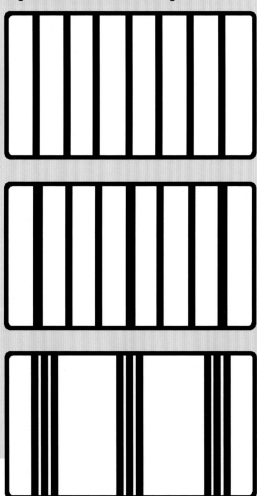

Unevenly spaced repetitions such as these below create an irregular rhythm. This feels more natural and adds visual interest to the composition through variety.

Translated into a shot, the regular rhythm used in the arrangement of figures makes the composition below feel strange and artificial. This could be effective for showcasing a mechanical or autocratic environment.

Distributing the figures in an uneven rhythm, as below, makes the composition feel more relaxed and natural. This kind of arrangement doesn't draw attention to itself and is effective for emotionally neutral shots.

Experimenting with a simple compositional setup shows how versatile rhythm can be. What kinds of adjectives can you generate by just playing around with the arrangement of three straight lines in a composition?

Calm

Chaotic

Boring

Dynamic

Decorative

Explosive

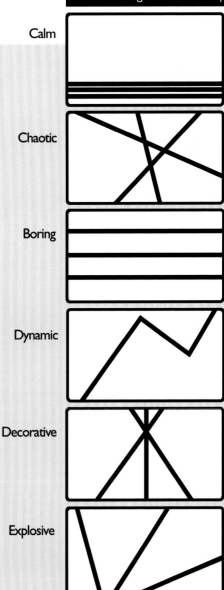

Now that you are aware of where lines occur in a composition and how they impact an audience, apply this knowledge when composing your frame. Design the structural lines in your image in such a way that they, through their orientation, quality and relationship to each other, further the mood and content of your shot.

Putting the concepts presented here to practical use will help refine your understanding of the theory. With practice, you will develop an intuitive understanding of the ideas discussed and develop your own unique approach to using them. Over time you will find that a few masterfully placed lines are all you need to design the most incredible shots.

# SHAPE
## COMING UP

# SHAPE

Stop looking at things in the frame as 'things' and you will see the composition break apart into a collection of shapes. The *nature* of these underlying shapes affects how we feel about what they represent and the frame as a whole.

Shape refers to any enclosed area created by an object, tone or color in an image. In film composition, this element plays a central role in the readability and emotional impact of a shot. Learning to control shapes will give you the ability to make the same mountain feel sharp and dangerous, flat and boring, or playful and inviting. In this chapter, we learn how to see these underlying shapes and how to design them to make your composition more dynamic.

Once you increase your awareness of shapes, you will notice that not only are these present everywhere in art and nature but can also, in themselves, carry a distinct emotional quality. A shape can be aggressive, calming, threatening, friendly, strong, gentle and so on, independent of what it is representing. Increasing our understanding of this emotional side of shapes is necessary to design compositions which go beyond being merely an appealing design and affect the audience emotionally. Nature, interiors, graphics, architecture and product design are all rich sources of material for interesting use of shape and should be mined constantly for inspiration and ingredients. As with lines, however, the first step to successful shape use is learning to see them from a compositional standpoint.

# DISCOVERING SHAPE

Underneath all the complexity in film frames, every good composition basically consists of a few well-designed tonal shapes. Before we learn how to use these for expression, we need to train ourselves to look past the detail, past the three-dimensionality and especially past our preconceived ideas regarding what we are seeing and focus on the underlying composition of shapes in the image. You may know a carpet to be rectangular, but the perspective, choice of lens, and play of light and shadow could be creating an entirely different set of shapes representing this carpet in the frame. Until this becomes second nature, ignore what something in a composition represents and focus instead on the abstract color and tonal divisions.

A composition is made of positive shapes and negative shapes. Positive shapes are composed of the darker tones and colors in an image while negative shapes are the lighter values or empty spaces that remain. These are equally responsible for defining the success or failure of a frame and the principles of good shape making apply to both.

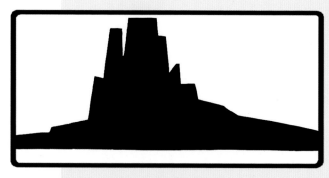

All compositions are made of a few basic shapes.

Simplifying variations in color and tone to a few basic values will give you the basis for dividing your frame into shapes.

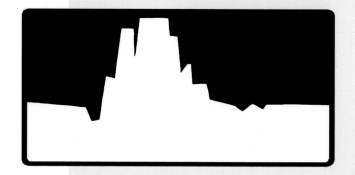

Shapes rarely present themselves in full graphic force in film frames or in real life, but can easily be distilled down to this.

The darker values are called positive shapes.

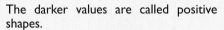

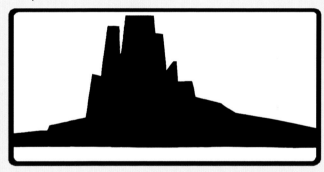

The empty space or lighter areas are called negative shapes.

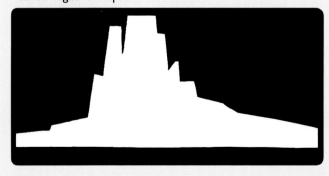

Pay attention to how the large blocks of tone are shaped in the frame. Get rid of unimportant details and simplify contours into broad representations.

These distilled compositions show different devices that can be used to design the structural shapes in an image. Negative space, light and shadow, foreground objects, organization of figures and angle of view are just a few ways a shot breaks up space to create an interesting compositional dynamic. Look for examples of good shape breakdowns in art as well as your surroundings. Increasing your awareness to the presence of shapes everywhere will result in a greater sensitivity and better aesthetic over time. When designing or analyzing compositions, pay special attention to the use of positivie and negative space in the frame. How the shapes in a composition relate to each other, as well as how they are designed and positioned individually, have an impact on the image.

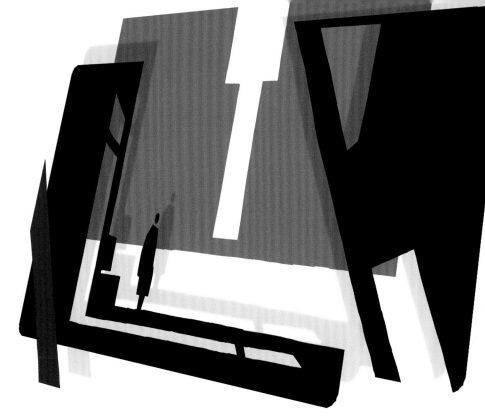

Seeing through this kind of a shape based mental filter helps you stay focused on the graphic breakdown in the frame. It is the interplay of shapes more that what they represent that matters at this stage.

Later chapters deal with additionally choosing the right motif to further the visual storytelling, but worrying about that right now would be putting the cart before the horse.

Having familiarized yourself with spotting major shapes in the frame, let's discuss the three principles that form the bedrock of great shape design: legibility, visual interest and emotional accuracy.

# LEGIBILITY

To begin with, a good shape needs to be legible. All the artistic interpretations in the world can be a bit hard to justify when at the end of the day the audience has no idea what they are looking at. In film, this takes on an even greater importance than in other media as here we are dealing with the additional component of time. Each shot has only a few seconds to communicate everything it needs to before we cut to the next shot. Any time the audience spends trying to decipher what a particular shape is, will be precious time away from whatever that shot was supposed to communicate in the first place. Designing shapes for quick readability is essential in film composition.

Often your frame will include only a part of an object, silhouette or stylized prop. In addition, we usually overlap one shape with another, creating depth and adding visual interest to the image.

# WHEN SHAPES ARE TOO BUSY, POORLY ARRANGED OR DESIGNED THEY RESULT IN SCARCELY READABLE IMAGES. SIMPLIFYING AND CLARIFYING CAN IMPROVE THESE CREATING THE QUICK READABILITY FOR FILM.

Analyze if the resulting shapes are still readable. Distance your mind from what you know a particular shape to be and objectively ask if a layperson would get this just by looking at the image. As visual storytellers, we need to constantly be mindful that we are trying to depict a whole world through the elements we put in the frame. For this to communicate, they have to be readable.

This is not to say that you should not use an atmospheric and lack of definition approach to composition, where appropriate. That is often the most effective way of generating mood and communicating certain story moments. The distinction which needs to be made is between deliberately ambiguous and accidentally unclear.

Deliberately ambiguous shots are the ones where one or a few shapes in the frame are partially obscured in some way to change the meaning of the shot or add a sense of mystery. For example, a low-key shot of a figure standing in the shadow might be surrounded by a dark shape in such a way that we cannot really make out it is a figure until there is movement. Here the lack of clarity is entirely planned, and will be resolved as the scene progresses.

Accidentally unclear on the other hand results in confusion rather than mystery and is a product of careless design and organization of shapes in the image. An example of an accidentally unclear shape would be anything that you want the viewer to recognize as one thing or another but unfortunately, due to poor placement and a weak silhouette, ends up just looking like visual confusion. Shapes that do not inform the viewer about what they are through their design will at best be ignored by your audience and at worst confuse them into misinterpreting the scene.

In order to ensure that shapes are legible, design the silhouettes to be clear and readable. If the shape is completely filled out in black, would the combination of positive and negative spaces within this graphic setup be sufficient to tell you what you are looking at? When you overlap one shape with another are they both still individually readable for what they are? Even collectively, the positive and negative shapes in the frame should be organized to make the composition more readable. In its simplest form this can be done by placing positive shapes against negative shapes and vice versa.

Finally, limit the number of major shapes in the composition to just three to five. The eye can only take in so much information at the same time. Always try and distill your composition down to whatever is most essential.

# VISUAL INTEREST

A defining feature of images with great compositional dynamic is that the individual shapes in them are visually interesting. Once you know how to spot them, it is amazing how clearly you can distinguish a shape that is visually interesting from one that is not. This factor can often make the difference between the same motif holding someone's attention or losing it. The key to making visually interesting shapes is variety.

Variety is foundational to the human experience. Imagine a world where everything and everyone look the same. The same colors, the same architecture, the same landscape at all times and in all places. Even beauty would become tasteless in such surroundings. Environments where everything is uniform and monotonous seem inhuman and cold. We need the stimulation of change in our visual experiences to keep things fresh and enjoyable. This same principle scaled down applies to our discussion on shapes.

Compositions with variety in the borders within a single shape as well as differences between the shapes in the image are more visually exciting than ones which have none. Variety in silhouettes, size differences, and distribution through the frame all heighten the visual drama in a shot. This variety makes for images which are more dynamic and hence better able to invite and hold audience attention.

For variety to be appealing, however, it must be tempered. Wild, disorganized, unrelated shapes with a lot of variation in them would possibly also create visual excitement, but hardly the kind you want. All contrast incorporated in a composition has to be balanced with factors like harmony and readability. This might take a little bit of practice, as you begin to understand how much variety for what scenario is 'too much' or 'too little'. Keep at it though and eventually it will become second nature.

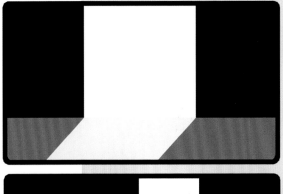

This is an example of one of the most boring shape breakdowns you can have in an image. The borders of the dominant white shape are identical in dimension and quality; poor integration between the elements results in the shapes just floating next to each other; and the position of the dominant shape is too central in the frame, considering nothing in the other elements breaks that symmetry.

Notice how the shapes behind the charater break up the space in uneven and visually interesting shapes. When composing, look for elements in your frame that you can use to break up the frame into interesting divisions.

This is slightly better because the height and width of the dominant shape are different and the asymmetrical arrangement results in more variety amongst the shapes.

This is now a visually interesting shape breakdown. The borders of the dominant shape have variety in quality as well as dimension and are well integrated into the other shapes in the frame. Though there is a nice diversity amongst the individual shapes, the composition still works as a cohesive whole.

The asymmetry and contrast the curtain shape injects in this composition adds tremendous visual interest to what would otherwise be an extremely lifeless image.

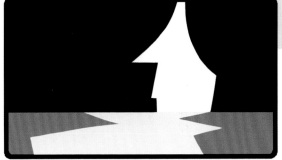

Here, the variety has been over-done. The shapes have lost their original integrity through too many variations on every side. Also, the absence of any one dominant shape, type or size results in the compositon not working as a single unit.

Despite differences, there are ways to make all the shapes in a composition feel like they belong to the same world. Tying a composition together with varying shapes that belong to the same shape family is an example of one such strategy. As with harmonious, complementary or split complementary color schemes, however, shapes which work well together can result from several aproaches to shape making. How much variety creates enough differences and what would be too much is ultimately a product of individual artistic judgement. The development of this judgement, however, can certainly be catalyzed.

Engage in constant analysis and experimentation in the play of shapes around you. Study how artists and filmmakers break up silhouettes and shape sizes to make a frame visually interesting. Experiment with abstract graphic compositions through thumbnailing or photography or focusing purely on the non representational aspects of the shapes used. What is the dominant shape in the frame? Does it have variety in the quality and dimensions of its borders? How about with the other shapes in the composition? Training your perception to recognize the ingredients of visually interesting shapes in successful images helps you understand how to create such shapes in your own shots.

A collection of shapes deriving from the same basic shape that contain slight variations in proportions and design are said to belong to the same shape family.

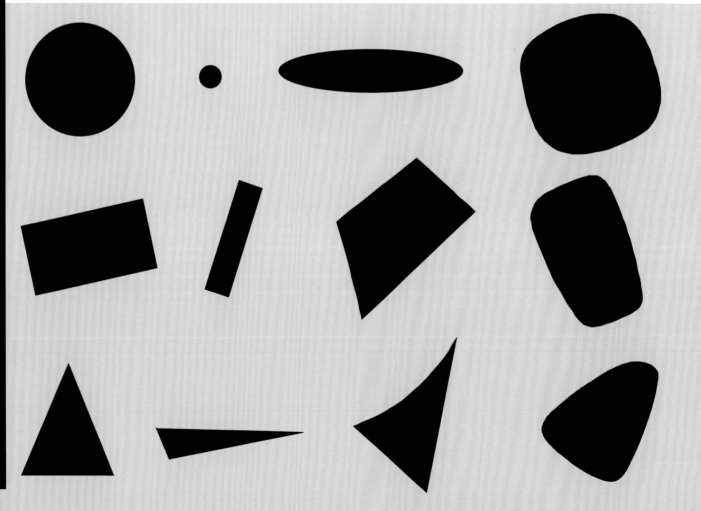

These usually make for harmonious compositions and can add variety within an image while still keeping the elements related.

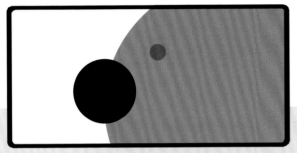

The repeating circles in this composition help tie the frame together, while the differences in size add interest to the image.

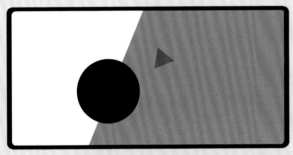

This composition contains shapes from entirely different families. In this case nothing is tying the elements in the frame together resulting in an image which lacks unity and appeal.

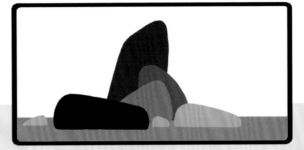

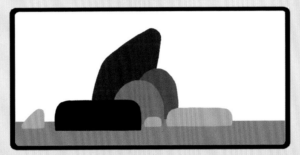

Shapes from the same family are easier to arrange into a harmonious design than shapes from several different ones.

Alternatively, shape families can be used to provide a backdrop to create contrast for a focal point in the frame. Notice how the circle in the image at bottom draws more attention that the rectangle in the image below.

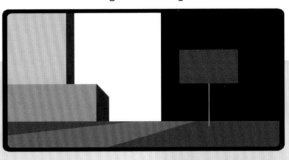

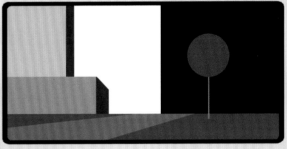

Once you understand the principle, shape families can be created using shapes with greater complexity integrated throughout the frame.

# SHAPING EMOTIONS

The types and size relationships of shapes in an image have a powerful effect on the mood of a composition. Certain kinds of shape and size contrasts inherently generate visual tension, while others reduce it. Designing the composition with this in mind — shapes woven into the underlying structure of a shot — can be used to visually amplify a story moment.

Abstract paintings often use shape dynamics to generate an emotional reaction even when the shapes represent nothing specific. The same dynamic can be applied to strengthening compositions dealing with actual locations and characters. For example, the negative space in the frame surrounding a character can feel a lot more threatening if composed of broken jagged triangles, than of rectangular or curved shapes. This could be created using set design or carefully positioning naturally occurring props in the frame. The basis for this effect is the concept of association discussed earlier in the psychology of images. Generally speaking, sharp shapes feel more dangerous than round shapes, as we associate sharp with menacing.

Beyond the nature of individual elements, harmony and contrast within different shapes also alter the feel of an image. Generally, compositions consisting of shapes from the same family, such as repeating rectangles in the skyline of a cityscape, add harmony to an image. Harmonious shapes can be effective for compositions which are based on beauty, decoration, serenity or a pattern-based design. These can make for very interesting visuals as long as some variety still exists within the similarity.

Contrasting shapes and sizes, on the other hand, increase the visual intensity of a composition. For example, extreme size differences increase the visual energy in a frame creating a greater sense of drama. A shot of a person standing next to a thick dominating pillar will generate a very different reaction from that of a person standing next to a thin elegant one.

Study art, architecture and nature — and analayze how the underlying shapes you see might be affecting you emotionally. Is it the type of shapes, size relationships, or harmony and contrast in the frame that is contributing the most to this feeling? Increasing your sensisitivity to this aspect of composition will expand your archive and make you aware of emotional applications of shape you never thought possible. Once you have grasped the basic idea, this concept can be used to tap into all kinds of associations.

The same basic motif projected using different types of shapes can result in very different emotional impacts. What would you say is the basic emotion of the scene in each of these compositions below?

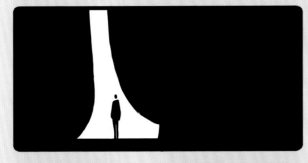

Here, the white square feels like it is dominating the frame.

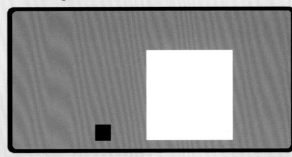

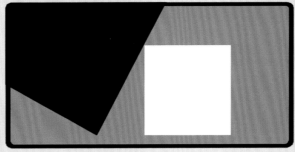

Here, the same white square feels like it is being overwhelmed by the larger dark square.

Fragmenting space creates contrast and energy in the frame, dramatically increasing its emotional intensity. When doing this, make sure the smaller shapes group together and subscribe to some larger pattern in the frame.

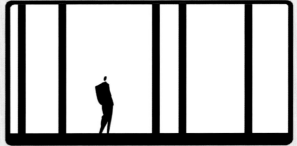

Even though they are basically portraying the same thing, these two shots feel very different. This is because of the changes in size relationships and repetitions in positive and negative shapes in the frame.

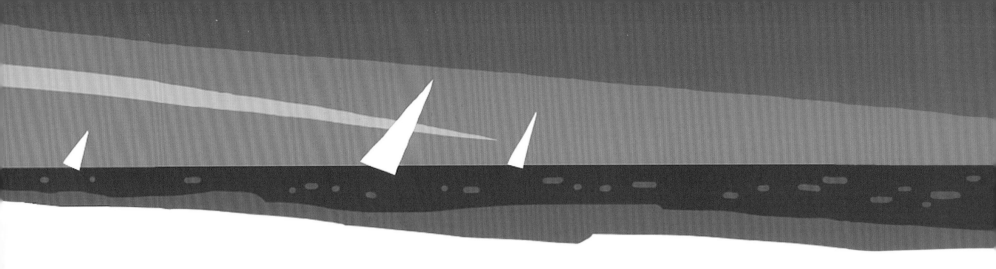

Take a few days to focus on the world around you wearing your shape 'lenses'. When sitting in a room, examine the type of shapes made by silhouettes and other noticeable tonal divisions. How does this connect to how the space feels? How would this feel if the shapes were a lot wilder or more caricatured? What if they were more toned down and had less variety in silhouette and size? Ask yourself those questions when walking around the city, admiring paintings and even observing people.

When watching a film, watch it on mute, pause on interesting shots and try to do quick thumbnail sketches which will help you see the breakup of big shapes in the frame. Notice how filmmakers use light, foreground elements and overall framing to create a desired set of shapes in the frame. Ask yourslf the questions from the paragraph above about these as well. Evaluate your own work to try to identify places where you can borrow some of these ideas to push the use of your shapes in the frame.

# VALUE

Value is how light or dark something is in a composition. It is also sometimes known as tone. When it is desaturated, every color translates into an equivalent tone on the greyscale. We might think of most images as being made of color, but it is often this underlying black and white structure that has the greatest impact on clarity and mood in the frame.

Understanding the fundamentals of how tone works and how it can be used to better tell a story is crucial to designing shots which resonate with your audience. This section explores how controlling different aspects of value can be used to define the design and emotional impact of a shot. Let's begin by understanding how to see value.

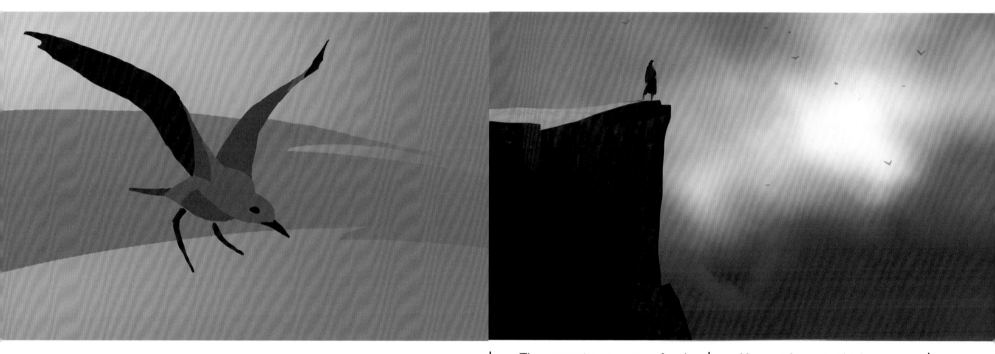

The narrative power of value has been used by visual storytellers since the beginning of the industry. Comics, illustrations and film all began by telling stories solely with black and white long before any of these mediums incorporated color. Unfortunately, this also leads people to underestimate the importance of learning how to work in black and white because it is perceived as something obsolete. This is a serious misconception.

You might not think you are watching a black and white movie when you go to your local cinema, but make no mistake: hidden underneath those thousands of shots in color lives a black and white structure that holds the cinematography together.

# SEEING VALUE

A greyscale refers to a progression through different shades of grey, going from white to black. The first requisite to mastering value is the ability to see a color and know where it fits on this chart.

value range

**lights          mid-tones          darks**

Training yourself to see value from a compositional standpoint is about two things: learning to look at a color and identify its position on a greyscale; and learning to simplify the value range of an image down to lights, darks and mid-tones.

Learning to accurately translate colors to their corresponding values on the greyscale can take time. Your perception needs to go through a sort of 'calibration' where you compare what you think the grey scale equivalent of a color is to what it actually is. You can practice this by making value studies from film frames and then using software like Photoshop to desaturate the images and compare. You will usually find a pattern in your mistakes. Maybe your lights are not light enough? Perhaps your mid-tones should really be darks? Make a note of which way you tend to lean and keep working on correcting course until your interpretations are accurate.

The second aspect to observing values is learning to simplify. In order to work successfully with tones, we need to establish a framework which allows us to process values in a manageable way. Condensing all the tonal complexities of an image into three broad categories of lights, darks and mid-tones allows us to capture the essence of a composition without getting lost in unnecessary detail. This tonal shorthand will allow you to quickly try different value schemes in a composition before committing to one.

Once you start to look at the world like this, you will find examples of tonal effects everywhere. When you start to see underneath the color, you will start to intuitively understand the patterns good compositions use and start incorporating them in your own shots.

An individual frame rarely uses the entire length of the scale. Every shot, or for that matter every part of every shot, has a certain value range. This consists of the length of the greyscale covered between the extremes of lights and darks used in this area.

Each value range, according to its own length and position, can then be further divided into lights, darks and mid-tones for that particular area or painting. The darkest tone in one painting might merely be a mid-tone on the actual greyscale, and the lightest patch in one part of a shot might be considered a dark with reference to the value range in a different area. Understanding, designing and following a good value range can make or break a composition.

Much like a musical octave, different notes on the scale can be combined to form value chords. Alternating the choice of what to use as lights, darks and mid-tones to form the value chord of an image will result in very different emotional impacts.

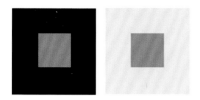

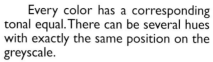

Value is relative. How dark or light a tone appears is as much a matter of the value surrounding an area as the value of the area itself. The grey squares in the center of both of these are identical. Yet, our perspective mechanisms lead us to believe that the one on the left is lighter than the one on the right, as it is surrounded by a darker value.

Every color has a corresponding tonal equal. There can be several hues with exactly the same position on the greyscale.

To think of values in a manageable way, compress the visual complexity in what you are trying to frame down to basic divisions of lights, darks and mid tones.

This process can also be reversed. When composing, first design a basic tonal sketch placing the major value divisions in the frame. Once you have experimented with this until you feel it is working for your story needs, start adding complexity in values and color without breaking the original value scheme created in your thumbnail. Learning to see the value structure of your frame on such a fundamental level will allow you to focus on the broad distribution of values before getting caught up in detail.

# VALUE DISTRIBUTION

Value distribution refers to the careful organization of lights, darks and mid-tones in the frame. Done well, this helps make the composition readable and balanced. Older live-action films contain some good examples of successful value distribution. Devoid of color, they offer an opportunity to understand how storytellers use value in their shot. Study these by reducing the composition down to three basic values, focusing on how the tones were distributed across the frame.

Another aspect of good value distribution is economy. Film compositions need to be instantly readable and should contain only the number of shapes on screen that the audience can grasp in a split second. This requires simplifying a vast number of individual elements in any given frame into three to five tonal shapes by organizing these elements into similar values.

Careful design of light, local color and framing is required to achieve this simplicity in the value distribution. Analyze your shots to make sure there are no redundant shapes or value changes. Ask yourself questions like: 'Does this white curtain in between this dark shape really add anything to the mood or content of the shot or is it just distracting from my focal point? Would it be better if I make it a grey curtain or have a shadow fall over the white curtain so it blends more into the larger area of dark that it is a part of?'

Do studies like the ones you see on the right to see how filmmakers you respect have approached similar problems.

# CONTROLLING FOCUS

The eye is attracted to the area of greatest visual difference between the light and dark tones in an image. Positioning this area of greatest tonal difference with deliberate intent allows us to control what the audience notices in the frame.

As a general rule, try to place the greatest difference in value at the point of interest in a scene. Attempt to create negative space around a character's acting area so that their actions are clearly set against a contrasting background. In the case of character or camera movement, try to reframe the scene in such a way that the greatest value contrast in the modified composition shifts to the new point of interest.

Tonal contrast is a relative concept. Depending on the value range in a composition, this could be as dramatic as a black shape inside a white shape, or as subtle as a mid-tone silhouetted against a lighter mid-tone. As your value range changes, the definition of contrasting values will change as well. For example, an extremely low contrast scene with a subtle value range like a ship in distant mists might take the tiniest tonal variation to attract audience attention, whereas a high contrast scene with a huge value range would probably take a much more significant difference in surrounding values to become a focal point.

Creating negative space around characters is a good way to create contrast in values while framing the action and making this the focal point of a scene.

Shifting the area of greatest contrast will change what the audience notices first. In this version, the painting holds more visual interest than the players. This concept can be applied to quickly draw the viewer's attention to a particular element in the frame.

It is not necessary to always use harsh contrasts to create significant focal points. Here, the character on the left gets noticed first even though he is only slightly lighter than other areas of the composition. Since tonal contrasts are relative, what constitutes enough contrast to draw the viewer's attention changes for every value range.

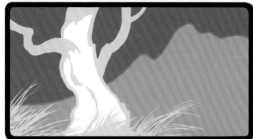

# VALUE PATTERN

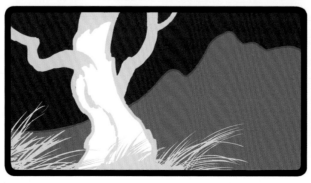

Compositions divided into clear foreground, mid ground and background layers are easier to read than compositions where this separation is not defined. One way to establish distinct visual layers in the frame is grouping each level of depth into a different value range. Perhaps your foreground and background is made of darks; and light values only exist in the mid ground? Perhaps your character stands out in the foreground as a light element with all the elements of mid ground and background falling away into darkness? You should have subtle variation within each layer to create interest, but make sure the contrast does not break the range you have set for that level of depth in the frame.

# VALUE and EMOTION

The tonal quality of a scene has a powerful impact on how it makes an audience feel. Tapping into some of our most primitive instincts, values use our fundamental associations with light and dark to visually showcase any action or event with an emotional undertone.

Whether achieved through a particular lighting situation, set design or stylistic treatment, the final tonal output of a composition draws its power from two main aspects of the value structure — the choice of the dominant tone in the scene, and the range and type of contrasts present.

Choosing the dominant value is the first decision you make regarding the tonal design of a shot. Should your frame basically consist of a dark background with a few lighter values or would a predominantly white background with small quantities of darks be more appropriate? Each of these choices will create a completely different mood for your shot and should be considered carefully.

Generally speaking, a shot that is enveloped by darker values tends to make a scene feel heavier, more serious and even threatening. This kind of value dominance is ideal for compositions that need to provoke a sense of danger, drama or fear. An interior of a haunted castle, for example, would be much more effective if composed of darker values than the other way around. Used a different way, dark values can also be effective to showcase things which involve other kinds of mystery, such as magic or romance.

Lighter values, on the other hand, are associated with purity, peace and divinity. As lighter values tend to calm the visual mood of a composition, dominance of these is best used for shots that are less dramatic and show-case a positive or relaxed story moment. A scene depicting a happy emotion such as a child playing, for example, would work well with light value dominance.

This way, even when you surprise audience expectation by using all the exceptions in the world, you are still operating with knowledge and understanding rather than with hopeful guesswork.

Next to the dominant value, the nature of contrasts in the tonal range also has a significant impact on the mood of a shot. Stark contrasts tend to generate a lot of visual energy and scenes with extreme differences between the lights and darks feel dynamic, dramatic and high tension. A climactic fight between two warriors would be a good example of where to use such a value range. Low contrast scenes on the other hand tend to be a lot quieter. Having a gentle and soft visual mood to them, such contrasts are effective for scenes with a subtle or subdued story moment. Sad emotions, such as a character grieving, often work very well with this value range.

As you go about familiarizing yourself with these principles, keep in mind that it is not that you cannot have dark scenes with happy emotions or bright, low-contrast scenes depicting a dangerous twist. Exceptions can be powerful when used with mastery. Whether you choose to follow the norm, abandon it, or turn it on its head though, you must understand a rule before you know how to break it.

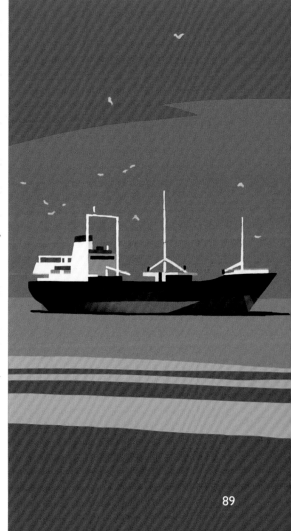

Spend some time analyzing values in art and real life. Watch black and white films as well as color films and do value studies simplifying how the tones are distributed across the frame. What is the dominant value in the frame? How does that affect mood? How would this change if the shot was a lot lighter or a lot darker overall?

Analyze your own work from a value perspective. Is the focal point the place of greatest value contrast in the frame? Does the value structure of the composition allow for a quick read of the shot? Are there any redundant shapes or values that can be blended into other values or shapes? Once you spend enough time squinting your eyes at images and doing studies in black and white, you will find you develop an 'x-ray like' vision which can instantly identify the value structure underneath an image and spot any problems it may contain.

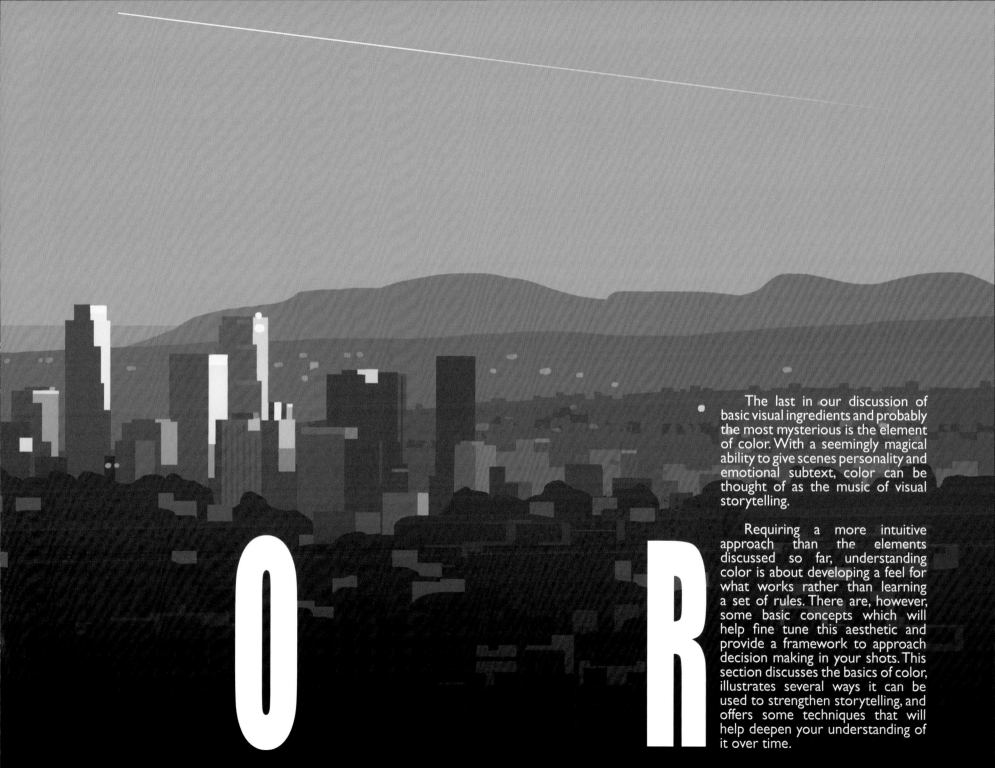

The last in our discussion of basic visual ingredients and probably the most mysterious is the element of color. With a seemingly magical ability to give scenes personality and emotional subtext, color can be thought of as the music of visual storytelling.

Requiring a more intuitive approach than the elements discussed so far, understanding color is about developing a feel for what works rather than learning a set of rules. There are, however, some basic concepts which will help fine tune this aesthetic and provide a framework to approach decision making in your shots. This section discusses the basics of color, illustrates several ways it can be used to strengthen storytelling, and offers some techniques that will help deepen your understanding of it over time.

# COLOR IS EVERYWHERE

Take a few moments and study the colors around you. With the exception of a few natural objects, you will notice that there is almost always a reason why a particular color is used in a certain place. Perhaps it somehow assists with the function an object serves, like the bright red on a fire extinguisher making the item easier to locate. Maybe it adds to your overall aesthetic experience of a space, like using harmonious hues in walls and furniture. Or maybe it is meant to influence how you feel about the object, like a bright orange energy drink which somehow seems to visually fit what it is.

We are constantly making sub-conscious judgements about objects based purely on the colors we see. Making this a far more conscious process and becoming aware of connections between the choice of color and the impact it has on our perception is the first step towards understanding this element. The biggest education you can have about color is by paying attention to how it is used in the world around you. Analyze everything. Why was that color used over there? What effect does a color have on how you perceive that person or object? How does that color relate to others in its environment? Even in the case where something is not working, ask yourself why that is so. How can you shift some of the colors in a particular design or environment to make it better do what it is trying to do? Despite the differences based on our own cultural perceptions, there is still tremendous common ground on how your audience reacts to the use of color in the frame. This provides visual story-tellers with the chance to turn what would otherwise be purely superficial choices aimed at making something look pretty into making choices that further the story and character.

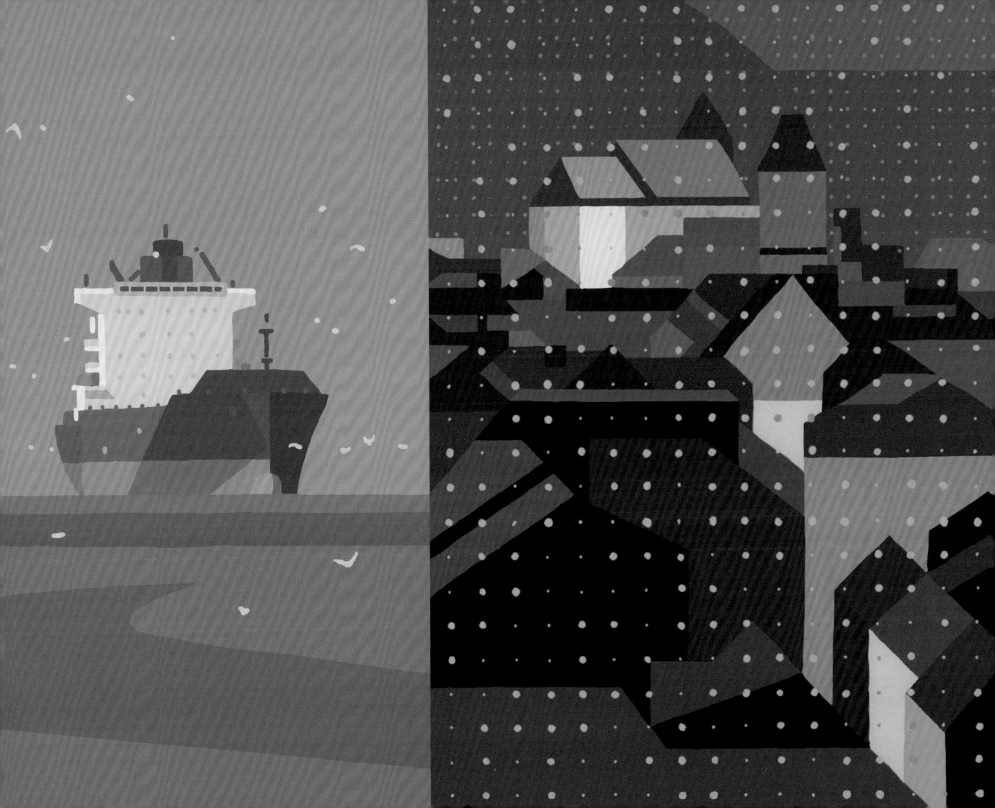

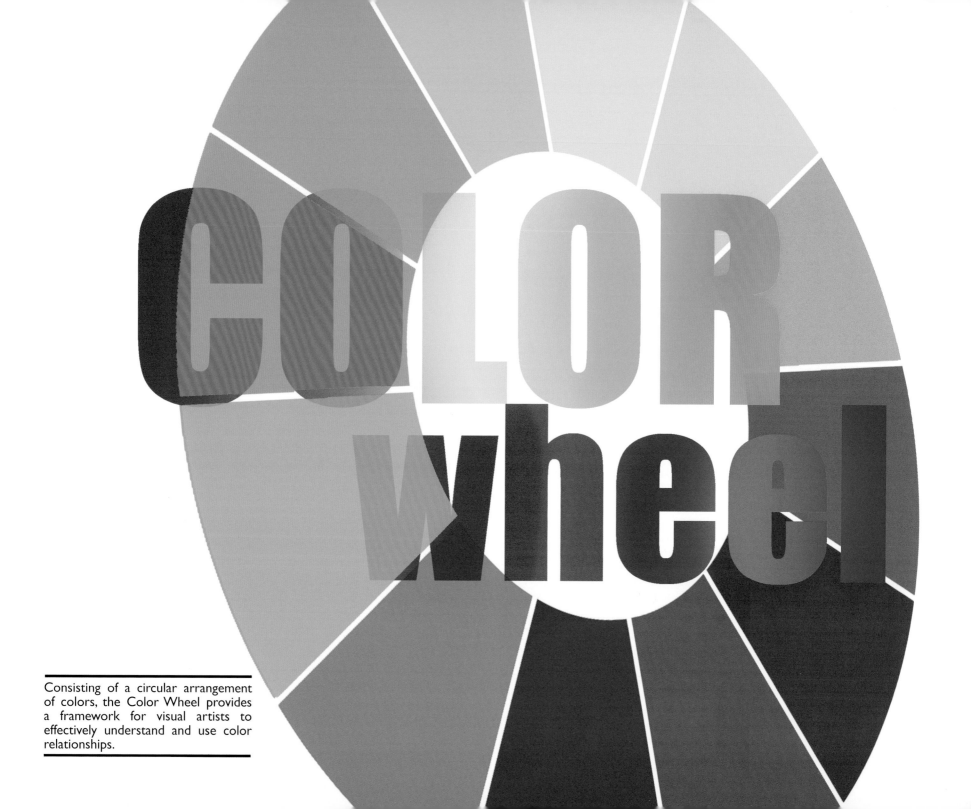

# COLOR wheel

Consisting of a circular arrangement of colors, the Color Wheel provides a framework for visual artists to effectively understand and use color relationships.

# HARMONIOUS COLORS

Colors that comprise of closely related hues positioned near each other on the Color Wheel. Orange and yellow are examples of harmonious color combinations.

# COMPLEMENTARY COLOR SCHEMES

Color schemes consisting of hues located on opposite sides of the Color Wheel. These have strong contrasts and increase the visual tension in a scene.

# ANALOGOUS COLOR SCHEMES

Color schemes consisting entirely of hues located along one side of the Color Wheel. These lack contrast and generally have a calming effect on the scene.

# COMPLEMENTARY COLORS

Colors that are positioned opposite to each other on the Color Wheel. Red and green are examples of complementary color combinations.

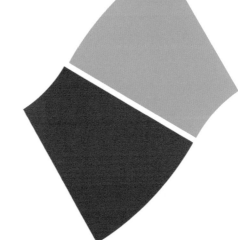

# A COLOR IS COMPRISED OF 3 PARTS

## HUE
## SATURATION
## BRIGHTNESS

| | |
|---|---|
| The root component of primary or secondary color. | **HUE** |
| The degree of intensity, vibrance or purity of hue. | **SATURATION** |
| The degree of lightness or darkness of the color. | **BRIGHTNESS** |
| Colors that look and feel relatively hotter, such as red, orange and yellow. Warm colors seem to advance and make spaces feel smaller or cosier. | **WARM COLORS** |
| Colors that look and feel relatively cooler, such as blue and green. Cool colors seem to recede and make spaces feel larger and more open. | **COOL COLORS** |
| Hues with large quantities of white mixed in them. | **TINTS** |
| Hues with large quantities of black mixed in them. | **SHADES** |
| Hues with large quantities of their complementary color mixed in them, making them very desaturated. | **NEUTRALS** |
| Color schemes consisting of just tints and shades of one single hue. | **MONOTONE** |
| Color schemes consisting entirely of black, white and neutrals. | **GREYSCALE** |

Having familiarized yourself with some basic color terms, try to spot them in the context of a shot. These two pages contain variations of the same basic motif with examples of the concepts already discussed. For instance, the image below is almost entirely composed of tints. Now try to match the correct terms to the rest of the color schemes.

A thorough understanding of the Color Wheel and basic color strategies is a must for all visual storytellers. With time, this will become second nature to the point that it acts as an automatic filter in your mind. Whenever you are confronted with a specific motif, you should be able to immediately visualize how it would look like in various color schemes. Even though you will still have to deal with problems that are unique to specific shots, this ability will assist your search significantly.

# PERCEIVING COLOR

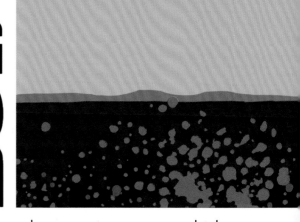

Simple as it sounds, identifying the hue with accuracy is often tricky enough by itself. One of the most fascinating aspects of colors is that they seem to change based on their surroundings. The examples on the next few pages show how the same color seems to appear completely different when placed next to a variety of other colors. You have to train yourself to isolate a particular color when dealing with an image and identify its base hue accurately even when it is significantly desaturated or shaded. With tools like Photoshop, this ability can be practiced, first by guessing a particular color in a photograph and then checking your guess against the results of an eye-dropper tool. Over time, your accuracy will grow, eventually becoming second nature.

Three things should be kept in mind when learning to see color from a compositional standpoint: identifying the hue with accuracy; learning to distill the composition into a few basic colors; and developing a system to store a particular color combination for future use.

composition is setting oneself up for failure. The solution is to train your mind to think in blocks or major divisions rather than every single color in a scene. When planning a composition, try to reduce the colors you are working with to a bare minimum. These should comprise the major divisions or families of color used, rather than

so you can remember it through a name such as yellow-orange. Regardless, find a system that allows you to quantify what a specific color is, so you can make a mental record of different color combinations you may want to use in the future.

The next aspect to perceiving color from a visual storytelling point of view is the ability to simplify. There are literally millions and millions of different colors. Trying to manage all of them when coming up with a

subtle variations within hues. Three to five colors are usually enough to capture the essence of a scene. Using this reduced palette, you can quickly try different combinations at the planning stage before you commit to one and start to flesh it out.

Finally, develop a technique to store color combinations for future use. Now that you have started to sensitize yourself to color, you will start to recognize examples of incredible color combinations constantly. Walking down the street one day you might see the most gorgeous blue sky set against a stunning white building that you feel captures the essence of summer. Find a way to remember this! No matter how clearly you might see it right now, your chances of recalling those exact colors some day in the future when you need to paint the perfect summer sky are dim at best. If you have a camera handy, take a photo and archive it in a way where you can find it when you need it. However, as visual language is your bread and butter, you should be able to remember colors even without a camera. People use all sorts of ways to do this. Some are as unique as remembering the specific feltpen marker numbers that are assigned to that particular color, so you can remember the series of numbers that will remind you of the colors you saw. Another example is to remember exactly where on the Color Wheel that color lies,

The endless number of colors nature contains can be rather difficult to keep track of when designing a shot. Whether you are trying to capture a scene from life or create an image from imagination, you must know which of the colors in question are the ones which matter.

REFERENCE PHOTO

REFERENCE PHOTO

Train yourself to distill the millions of subtle variations down to three to five colors that capture the essence of a composition. These simplified paintings are known as Color Keys and are used to explore different color schemes for a particular image.

COLOR KEY

COLOR KEY

Once you are satisfied with a direction, you can expand on them to create more subtlety.

## COLOR PALETTES / SWATCHES

Color palettes are like an 'ingredient list' for the color of an image. These two swatches are derived from the Color Keys, which in turn were derived from photographs. Do as many such studies as you can. Apart from developing a keen ability to identify the key players in a color scheme, you will also have handy access to a huge library of swatches capturing various color flavors.

# HOW LIGHT, DARK OR SATURATED A COLOR APPEARS IS RELATIVE TO THE COLORS SURROUNDING IT

Notice how the same basic color seems to glow when placed against a darker background and darken when placed against a lighter background.

Surrounding a color with a complementary or relatively desaturated hue will make a color seem a lot more intense than surrounding it with an analogous color with competing levels of saturation.

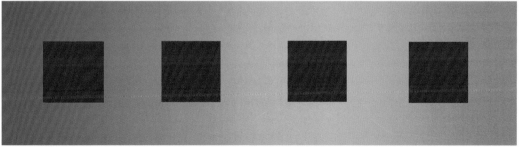

Pay close attention to this relative effect colors have on each other. Choosing the context for a color is as important as choosing the central color itself.

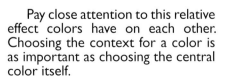

SOMETIMES, IN OUR OBSESSION WITH MAKING SOMETHING LOOK PERFECTLY 'ACCURATE', 'REAL' AND SUPER, MEGA, ULTRA 3D, WE LOSE TRACK OF SOMETHING IMPORTANT. WE FORGET THAT AT THE END OF THE DAY, WE ARE TELLING A STORY

# COLOR + EMOTION

What color are the walls of the room you are sitting in? How do you think the feel of this space would be affected if these were bright red instead? What if they were black? Though we usually remain completely oblivious to how our emotions are manipulated by something we are used to seeing, the color surrounding us has a deep impact on our state of mind.

For reasons both science and art have been trying to understand for hundreds of years, our emotions respond instinctively to color. Fields as diverse as design, advertising and even medicine often have entire departments dedicated to exploring and exploiting these qualities. While this emotional dimension is no doubt the most valuable function color serves in visual storytelling, it is probably also the most under utilized.

Despite advances in technology, more often than not film visuals today fail to engage the audience on an emotional level and resort instead to dialogue heavy scenes or visual extravagance to hold audience attention. Perhaps one of the reasons for this shortcoming lies in the technology itself. Sometimes, in our obsession with making something look perfectly 'accurate', 'real' and super, mega ultra 3D, we lose track of the story we are telling. Focusing on creating a visually believable world so that the audience can lose themselves in the narrative should certainly be part of your visual choices, but only one part. There are several ways in which the visualization of a scene can be 'accurate' — and emotional accuracy is as much, if not more, a part of good production design as any other kind.

**THE COLOR SURROUNDING US HAS A DEEP IMPACT ON OUR STATE OF MIND**

Fundamentally, there are two ways in which a color or color palette can affect our emotions. The first, based on harmonics, is a result of the visual energy created by how the colors relate to each other. Contrasting colors, such as red and green, increase the intensity of the frame and usually generate excitement or tension in the shot. Conversely, analogous colors such as yellow and orange act in unison with each other and make the visual more serene and harmonious.

# EMOTIONAL ACCURACY IS AS MUCH, IF NOT MORE, A PART OF GOOD PRODUCTION DESIGN AS ANY OTHER KIND OF ACCURACY

The second strategy color uses to generate emotion is based on association. The power of association through color is incredibly powerful and diverse, making it probably the strongest element to use for employing this concept. Associations can be used on a direct level, such as by using the association of red and blood in a certain scene to act as a trigger to generate a related emotion. But this is just the tip of the iceberg. Some of the greatest power associations in color come from indirect use, where you tap into the color scheme of a particular time, place, season, genre and so on to create the ideal atmosphere for a particular scene. This is indirect use of association.

Using the example of a house and some surrounding landscape, the next few pages show how much variety can be achieved in what a shot communicates by simply changing the color scheme used in the frame.

# GETTING EMOTIONALLY

If we were to give a computer the job of translating a photograph into a painting, a feature available in several software programs, all it would produce is an image based on the 'averaging' of colors. The feel of the original and any emotional subtext in the source, in all probability, would be lost. This is because successfully picking colors from any reference is not fundamentally a mechanical process. It is an emotional one.

Distilling color is a deeply conscious and creative undertaking. Picking one color means rejecting a lot of others and the art is no different from that of an editor trying to refine the tone and content of a message. The three to five colors that best capture the essence of a visual may not necessarily by the three to five colors which appear in the greatest quantity. Finding the essence is a sensitive process. How successful you are at it will depend ultimately on how emotionally tuned in you are to what you are doing.

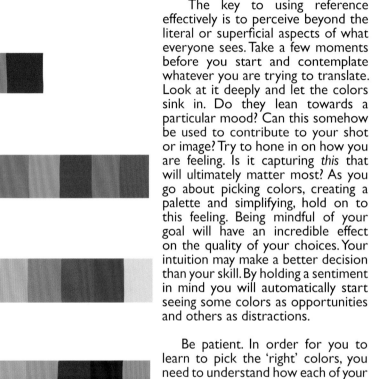

The key to using reference effectively is to perceive beyond the literal or superficial aspects of what everyone sees. Take a few moments before you start and contemplate whatever you are trying to translate. Look at it deeply and let the colors sink in. Do they lean towards a particular mood? Can this somehow be used to contribute to your shot or image? Try to hone in on how you are feeling. Is it capturing *this* that will ultimately matter most? As you go about picking colors, creating a palette and simplifying, hold on to this feeling. Being mindful of your goal will have an incredible effect on the quality of your choices. Your intuition may make a better decision than your skill. By holding a sentiment in mind you will automatically start seeing some colors as opportunities and others as distractions.

Be patient. In order for you to learn to pick the 'right' colors, you need to understand how each of your inclusions affects your composition visually as well as emotionally. Mastering this takes time. Do as many such studies as you can. Apart from developing a keen ability to identify the key players in a color scheme, you will also have handy access to a huge library of swatches capturing various color flavors.

It is also useful to have some sort of system by which you arrange your palette. A methodical approach towards color simplification will make the act of doing this simpler as well. One such way is to first identify the lightest hue which you feel plays a significant part in the composition. Once you have this, find the next significant color which is close to it in the Color Wheel. For example, if your lightest hue is a light yellow, and light orange is also used, put this next to the yellow. Following the same process, slowly make your way round the Color Wheel getting all the representational colors step by step. You will find by the end that not only have you covered the entire range quite thoroughly, but also that your palette itself will be a pleasing design. Whether you use this approach or not, you need a system. Making efforts to establish good habits in these early stages pays dividends later.

# INVOLVED

Creating compositions with appealing color combinations is ultimately based on the same principles we have explored so far with the other elements of design. Unity, variety, balance and so on. The difference, as mentioned before, is that color is a lot more intuitive.

Let's say you are trying to create a soothing composition for a calm scene. You decide to use cool colors that are harmoniously located next to each other on the Color Wheel. This theoretical approach will only narrow things down to blue and green. However, there are millions of 'blues' and 'greens' and though they should be technically harmonious, some of them look terrible together! On the contrary, certain colors with no logic to belong to each other may look stunning with each other! You should know, intuitively, when something looks good and when it does not.

This is where patience and hard work come in. Spending time looking at and studying good work is probably the fastest way to refine your aesthetic and develop that sense of judgement. This is why apprentices in the old artistic tradition did reproductions of Old Masters' works. When you copy something with a conscious focus on learning from the process, you will imbibe some of who you are copying into your own artistic DNA.

The good news is you are already on the right track. Having by this point studied value, you have taken the best first step towards creating a sound color composition. You know by now how to create clearly established focal points, some

degree of balance, and value based contrast and unity. Now you have to translate that tonal structure into corresponding hues without undoing any of your work so far.

Many concepts we discussed in the basics of good value design can also be applied to color. For example, try to have one overarching dominant hue that ties the rest of the variety in the composition into one unified whole. Not having a clearly established dominant hue will result in the composition feeling scattered. Limit the number of different hues you use. Masterpieces have been painted using just a couple of hues while paintings with every color from the wheel simply don't work. As you balance lights and darks in an image, so you should warms and cools. Warms against cools, and cools against warms, make for strong focal points and clear legibility.

You will come to realize that colors are more about relationships than individual colors. Always be aware of the big picture. Several of the incredible effects that color can achieve are rooted in this relationship between a color and its surrounding color. Take, for example, the term 'making a color sing'. This refers to designing the colors in the environment of your focal point 'star color' in such a way that it provides the maximum vibrance. Think of the blocks that seemingly changed color based on what was surrounding them. When designing the background color in a scene, always relate it to the color of your focal object/character and how you want it to blend in or stand out with the rest of the scene.

# COLOR AND DESIGN

The first step to designing good color is good values, so study the chapter on values first before tackling color. A good tonal plan for a successful color composition has clear value dominance, balanced distribution of values, and a clear focal point.

This is an example of a mistranslated value scheme. The color here has not maintained the integrity of the original tonal arrangement with colors becoming darker or lighter than the values dictated. This changes the composition's focal points and balance and should be avoided, until you have first mastered the ability to step through from value to color.

Here, the tonal scheme has been accurately translated, but too much variety in hues has rendered the composition ugly. Lack of dominance in hues and an over abundance of colors has made this composition impossible to unify.

# COLOR AND VALUE

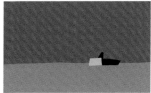

This example successfully translates the value into an appealing color scheme. Using just a few colors in more or less the same part of the Color Wheel, this shot makes for a unified image with clear dominance and harmony. This goes to show how even the most limited number of hues used well can make a successful color scheme.

Another successful translation from values, here the color scheme is complementary. An additional strategy used in this composition is of opposing color temperatures. The cool background clearly separates the land in the distance from the warm foreground. This creates visual energy, balance and a sense of depth in the image. Generally speaking, cools tend to recede while warms advance.

By now you should have a fair idea of how powerful color can be if used meaningfully in visual storytelling. Good color generates beauty, conveys information and heightens emotion. The houses on the previous pages illustrate several ways color reference from a variety of areas can be used to communicate subtext about a scene. Let us delve a little deeper into some of the strategies and associations these examples use.

Over the next pages we explore how color is used in visual storytelling to give information regarding the season, weather and even time of day to heighten the narrative experience. We see how different parts of the world have distinctive color flavors and how different genres of cinema use this element.

Concepts explored here are simply some 'quintessential' color schemes most closely associated with the specific areas. Certainly, it is possible to find all kinds of color arrangements in all sorts of circumstances, but not all of these are representative of specific categories. Color archetypes are a great way to benefit from the powerful association which people have with certain locations, seasons, weather conditions and genres to make for a more powerful visual.

Finally, it must be said that this should only be treated as a mere initiation into the immense world of color. There is no sure shot formula to be followed or final word on the subject. Ultimately, observation from life will be your greatest teacher. The aim of this section is to simply make you aware of the abundance of levels on which color operates and can be used to improve the storytelling.

# THE POWER OF COLOR

**HAPPY STYLIZED**

**ICE COLD WINTER EVENING**

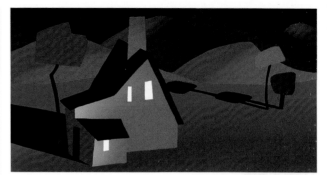

**HOT, BATTLE**

**WILD WEST**

**WARM SUNSET**

**FILM NOIR**

**SNOWY WINTER AFTERNOON**

**EARLY SPRING MORNING**

**COLD AUTUMN**

**FOGGY EVENING**

**HEAVY SPRING SHOWER**

**FULL MOON**

**AUTUMN NIGHT**

**EARLY FOGGY SUMMER MORNING**

**CONFLICT SITUATION**

**AUTUMN MORNING**

**SNOWY WINTER NIGHT**

**ARTIFICIAL TINT**

**ROMANTIC MOOD**

**HOT SUMMER NOON**

**SNOWSTORM**

**EERIE**

**CHILDREN BOOK STYLE**

**HORROR**

Think about how much power the weather has to shape how you feel every day. How much does your perception of a dull overcast day differ from a bright sunny one? As with seasonal color schemes, weather-based color schemes also offer a tremendous opportunity to tap into your viewers' memories and life experiences to further the emotional goals of the story.

Since the weather dictates the quantity and quality of light as well as visibility in the environment, it is a defining factor for the color in a scene. An overcast day, for example, would desaturate all hues and project a sense of gloom in the frame. Conversely, a sunny day with its bright light would showcase the variety of colors and make for a more upbeat and energetic scene. Blizzards, rain, sandstorms, lightning, fog, snowfall and so on all make for a very distinctive visual and emotional fabric and should be studied for the unique color possibilities they offer.

Having a weather-heavy scene can also add greatly to the visual appeal of your frame. This is because most strong weather conditions tend to simplify the tones, colors and even focal points in an image, making for a much more unified composition. For example, an environment with an establishing shot of a small village in Europe with a chaotic arrangement of unharmonious colors might well make for a stunning vista if shrouded in mist with only a few shapes and silhouettes coming through.

Take the time to explore unusual weather conditions and the color scheme possibilities they offer in a shot. Finding a situation which is appropriate from a narrative as well as a design standpoint can greatly amplify the visual and emotional power of an image.

# LOCATION

Different geographical locations often have a very distinctive color palette. Chinese culture, for example, uses a lot of bright, warm, saturated reds and oranges, while a certain blue and white scheme can immediately be identified as Mediterranean. When location needs to be established, or the geography is significant to the story, tapping into these quintessential color schemes helps trigger associations and place the viewer.

Environments like rain forests, deserts, ocean floors and so on also have distinctive color schemes. Researching and using the actual colors found in these environments brings tremendous authenticity to the frame and enhances the viewer's experience of the story. Don't settle for the generic color schemes. Finding reference for the environments will make you aware of opportunities you couldn't dream up.

Color from locations can also be used very effectively in unusual ways. For example, taking the specific colors found in the underwater world and using them to paint the flora and fauna of a jungle can be effective in creating the feel of an 'alien' forest. Color schemes found in one location and consciously used to subvert or manipulate audience expectations in unusual ways can be a great way to create interesting visuals.

Nothing beats travel to familiarize yourself with the variety found in the visual world. Additionally, you should try to get as much exposure as possible to the art histories, cultures and geographies of places around the world. This will enable you to draw from a vast reservoir of knowledge when you are trying to pick the appropriate color palette for a given location.

# DAYTIME

Another factor largely responsible for defining the colors in a scene is the time of day it is shot. The quality, color and strength of light is constantly changing throughout day and night. Understanding these characteristics and learning how to use them allows us to replicate the appearance of a specific time and gain an appreciation for how much an environment can transform visually and emotionally over a single day.

Morning hours usually consist of softer light and colors as the cooler thicker air, combined with more atmospheric diffusion, causes the sunlight to appear as a tint of yellow on a cloudless day and slightly cooler on a cloudy day. As the sun moves up in the sky the situation changes. Afternoon light is harsher and generally white in color. Since it is a strong source of white light lighting everything, it can be challenging to unify all the hues in

a scene. The 'magic hour' before the sun sets is often considered to be 'prime time' by photographers. The light at this time has a lovely golden quality which unifies and saturates the compositions, additionally giving the beautiful backdrop of a sunset. These saturated warm hues often work well for romantic moments. Night time, of course, brings with it an entirely new set of hues and variations, depending on the moon and cloud cover.

Picking the right color scheme and capitalizing on the appropriate time of day will not just add a certain degree of believability to your frame, but also allow you to access the inherent symbolism which viewers associate with concepts of sunrises, sunsets and so on.

127

GENRE

Over time, certain color schemes have become closely associated with a particular genre of cinema. For example, musicals tend to have theatrical visuals 'caricaturing' emotions through use of bold and saturated colors. Documentaries, on the other hand, usually rely on naturalistic or found colors so as to portray the reality of a situation. Using these familiar color schemes can put the viewer in the appropriate frame of mind to receive the kind of information which that film is communicating.

Think about the different color schemes which come to mind when, in turn, visualizing horror films, film noir, science fiction, mysteries, comedies, and so on. Pay attention to the predominance of certain hues, tints and shades in a given genre. How does this contribute to how you feel about the image? How can you use this to further your narrative goals?

Genre-based color schemes should be used with extreme caution. Relying solely on a formulaic approach to colors without having them integrate with the story in some original way makes for dull and lifeless compositions. Always look for an opportunity within the script, location or story moment which makes it possible to cater to certain color schemes.

SEASONS

Different seasons offer unique visuals and emotions. A beautiful spring day immediately brings to mind images of bright flowers, saturated colors, and an overall feeling of vibrancy, energy and positivity. Contrast this with what a bleak winter day might conjure in your mind. By using specific color schemes that are related to different seasons, we are able to tap into the mental and emotional associations and memories which already exist in the viewer's psyche.

In order to successfully capitalize on seasonal color schemes, you would require a script which take this dimension into consideration. The colors have to be appropriate to the story progression and used only in specific points in the narrative in order to direct the audience's emotions.

Study the visual, emotional and symbolic qualities of various seasonal color schemes. The reds and oranges of autumn, the desaturated shades of winter and the bright saturated colors of summer all lend very different flavors to your composition. Explore the various ways in which these can be used to further your visual storytelling. Keep in mind that the same season can also offer several color variations. For example, winter staged from a 'holiday Season' perspective would focus more on the contrast between the warm colors of indoor fires with the cool blues of the outdoor snowy landscape. On the other hand, a wintry scene that depicts a 'cold, barren environment' would be better expressed by focusing on shades of grey and desaturated tones which offer very little contrast and visibility.

# COLOR SCRIPT

## S T E P S

A Color Script is a series of basic color thumbnails done to define how the color transitions over the course of a narrative. Images done for a Color Script are known as Color Keys, and should be by definition very reduced. These need only have an indication of the staging and compositional elements in a shot and should focus instead on exploring the best combination of two to five basic colors which broadly define the mood of a scene.

When doing a Color Script, the first step is to thoroughly mine the story for information. What are the major themes in this narrative? Which are the significant turning points in the script? What are the major locations? How about times of day and weather conditions in different scenes? How is the story line structured and paced? What are the subtexts? Which character's point of view are different scenes shot from? Ultimately, you will need to combine the answers and ask the most significant question color needs to satisfy: how should your audience feel at a given point in the story?

## Mood Curve

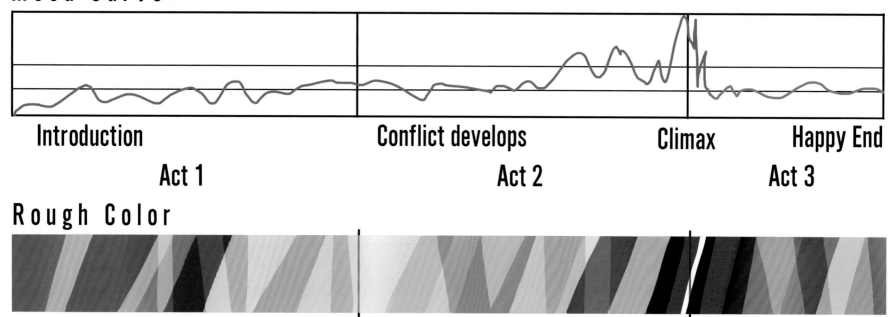

Introduction

Conflict develops

Climax

Happy End

Act 1

Act 2

Act 3

## Rough Color

Act 1

Act 2

Act 3

# Color Keys

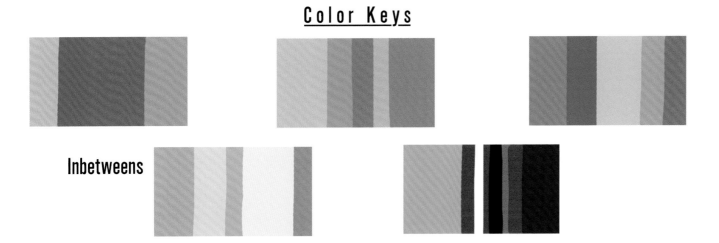

Inbetweens

Once you have jotted down these notes on the script and understood clearly the emotional goals for the color in your film, you can approach your first Color Key. One effective place to start is to establish the color scheme for a neutral or 'normal' moment in your film. Different films can have very different neutrals. Film noir, for example, might have a much darker neutral than a comedy. It is important to establish what your film's 'normal' is first, so you know what your point of departure is when trying to visualize a dramatic or subdued story moment. Even if you eventually replace this key with one which is more specific to a moment in the story later, it is important to start with this step.

Having designed a basic two to five color Color Key which represents the neutral of your story's color range, you will now block in the extremes. Pick what you feel is the most intense or dramatic story moment in your script. Remember, these don't always come at the climactic end; sometimes it will be in the second act. Keeping in mind your neutral, pick the most intense color scheme which you feel could still belong in the visual world of the story. This has to be sufficiently compelling visually to do the dramatic story point justice, but not so jarring that it breaks the visual fabric of the film. Again, different genres have different degrees of flexibility. Once this is done, bearing in mind your extreme and neutral Color Key, you key out the colors for the most subdued moment in your film. Think of this like establishing the tonal range in a composition.

When these major milestones are mapped out, you can start to fill in the chunks in between. Keep in mind factors like locations, times of day, and continuity requirements which will force you to make some color choices at points in the script. Maybe some colors will be reserved for certain characters or locations; maybe some for repetitive story elements. The most decisive factor, however, should remain the emotional component. Any given situation provides tremendous amounts of opportunity to create circumstances which allow for the kind of light or color which your scene requires. Discuss these with the director to see if anything can be incorporated into the story.

The quality of transitions from one color scheme to the next are also significant factors in Color Keys. Depending on the mood and story moment, some color changes might be ushered in gently, introducing one color at a time into the previous key until it blends seamlessly into the new color scheme. Other times, you might wish to jar the audience by dramatically changing the color completely from one scheme to the next. Keep in mind also that colors will feel different depending on the order in which they appear. Contrasts also have a temporal component. Complementary colors in connected shots, for example, will create more visual contrast and excitement the same way as they would if used together in a single image.

Traditionally, one tends to have reds and greens associated with danger; pinks and violets with love; and so on. These stereotypes can be effectively used in a film, but also be played with. You could create new associations by repeatedly pairing some colors with certain kinds of events in the story, but do this with caution as it can feel a bit like going against the grain. Value, of course, needs to be deeply considered when creating a Color Script, as it defines the underlying skeleton of the color scheme. This has been dealt with in another chapter.

Feedback is a necessary part of this process. Ultimately, this is only one approach to creating a Color Script for your narrative. Over time, your individual personality and story requirements might dictate a more personalized approach. The important thing to keep in mind, regardless, is that color be used not merely as a decorative element. The Color Script should reflect the world of the story and enhance the audience's experience of the narrative.

# COLOR SCRIPT

This is part of a Color Script for the 30min short *The Cold Heart*. As you can see, all sequences blend colorwise into the next ones.

There are a few breaks where the color changes abruptly because of major story turns. In general, the transitions between sequences are smooth and barely noticeable.

**N**ow that you are aware of the several dimensions which color can be used to achieve, there is simply no excuse for accidental or thoughtless use of color when composing the palette for your shots. Using color to merely make for pleasing compositions is completely insufficient for the purposes of visual storytelling. A pleasing color combination can be achieved in any circumstance. You must strive to go beyond this mere first level of successful color and additionally use it to convert information about the story and amplify emotion.

Ignoring these qualities will simply make for weaker visuals. Now that you have some exposure to the tremendous informational and emotional potential that each color in your frame contains, it should come as no surprise that failure to pay attention to this department could well mean that you are confusing the audience by sending out misleading signals through accidental color choices.

Subverting expectations done consciously, however, is a completely different thing. Often you are aware of the dynamics of color and the associations they bring, so you can use this knowledge to trick the audience! For example, a horror-type lighting can be used to raise audience anticipation, apprehension and excitement, only to end up being an anticlimactic, funny moment. Conversely, having something extremely dramatic happen in naturalistic lighting might be used to increase shock value, since lack of color cues takes away the viewers' opportunity to brace themselves. The point is that once you are aware of how the audience will be reading the color information and emotion in a scene, you are in a position to give them an interesting ride, whether you subvert or fulfill their expectations.

Finally, don't try to stuff each and every concept you have learnt into each and every composition. This can be overwhelming and result in confused color schemes which are trying to do so much they accomplish nothing. You will often find that simply picking the appropriate choice in one area, such as location, season, weather or emotion, will automatically allow for the remaining areas to fall into place. Keep it simple and always focus on a result oriented approach. If, at the end of the day, it works visually and emotionally, it works!

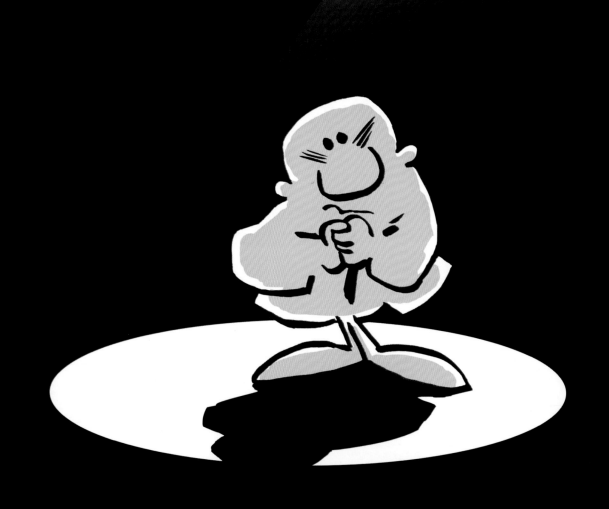

# light
## NEXT

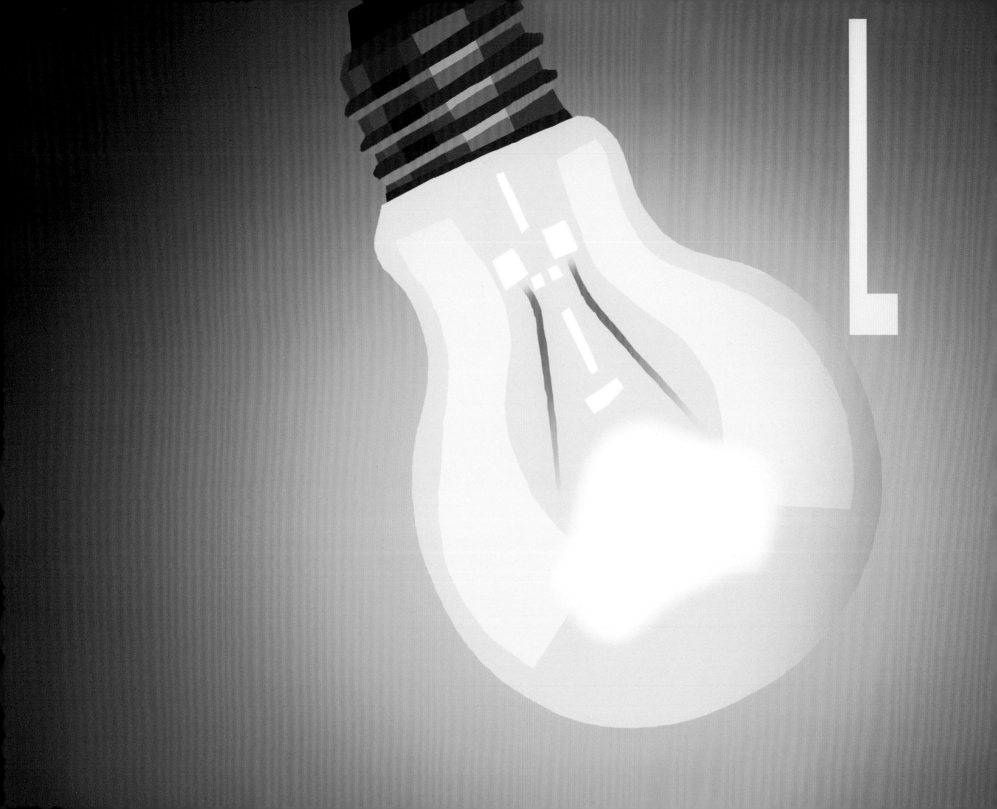

# i g h t

Light is one of the most powerful visual storytelling tools at our disposal. Regardless of whether you are using actual light shooting in real life, 'digital light' simulated through a software, or conceptual light while composing an illustration, the fundamental principles remain the same.

This chapter deliberately ignores the 'physics' of light, a subject covered by many books on the market, and focuses instead on the narrative aspects. We explore the many dimensions of light and how these can be manipulated to generate mood, organize the frame, and control value and color in a shot. Understanding light from a storytelling point of view will make your compositions more emotionally and visually compelling irrespective of the medium.

Right now, wherever you are, the light in your environment is influencing your world. It is altering the colors you see, defining visibility, possibly creating some focal points and affecting how you feel. For something which is itself invisible, light has a singularly incredible ability to shape the visual fabric of a space.

As a visual storyteller, you need to know how this works: to be acutely aware of the different types and aspects of light; to understand what they do visually and emotionally; and to recognize opportunities in a shot to use this to your advantage. The first and most important step is the same as that of mastering any visual component: start paying attention to the world around you.

Become a student of light. Notice it wherever you go. Study how it is used in interiors, architecture, film frames, painting, photography and wherever else you come across it. Train yourself to look at a composition and reverse engineer the kinds of lights used, their placement, and possible reasons for the designers making those choices. Start making a mental archive of different lighting situations. What are the visual qualities and emotional associations that go with each of these? Sunlight, moonlight, candlelight, neon lights, spotlights, street lights, flood lights, night lights... the list is endless! As will be the number of ways that you will eventually learn how to use these in your compositions.

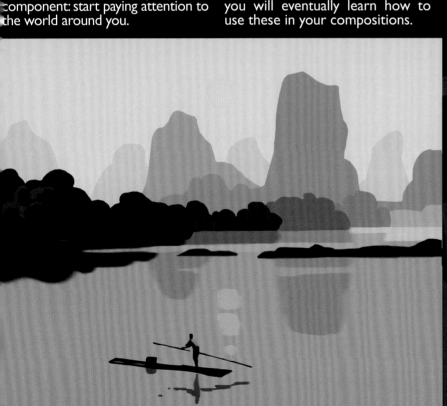

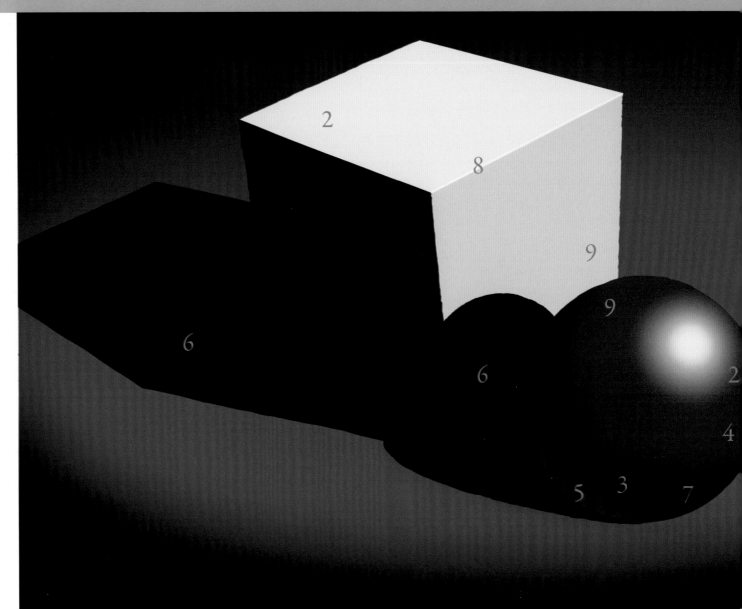

## BEFORE WE START EXPLORING THE USE OF LIGHT FOR VISUAL STORYTELLING, WE NEED TO UNDERSTAND THE DIFFERENT ELEMENTS INVOLVED IN A BASIC LIGHTING SETUP.

**1** **Light Source** — Where the light is coming from in a scene. In case light from the sun is passing through a curtain before entering the scene, then the luminous curtain is considered the light source. There are generally several light sources in a given scene, but a principal light source has the largest visual impact.

**Light Color** — The color of light.

**Strength** — The amount of light radiating from the light source.

**Direction** — The positioning of the light source with respect to the subject. Eg, this ball is lit from back three fourth.

**Quality** — The kind of light emitted by the light source. Light sources can be harsh, such as a torch or headlight, or extremely soft and diffused, such as through a curtain.

**2** **Highlight** — The brightest point on an object's surface where the light hits most directly.

**3** **Falloff** — The rate of change from the lit side of an object to the dark side.

**4** **Object reflectivity** — The surface quality or 'shininess' of the object. Objects with different reflectivities react very differently to light.

**5** **Reflected Light** — Indirect light illuminating the shadow side of an object by bouncing off other surfaces.

**6** **Cast Shadow** — Cast shadow is the shadow thrown by an object onto other surfaces such as the table it is on, or nearby objects.

**7** **Core Shadow** — The darkest part of the shadow which occurs next to the edge between the lit side and shadow side of an object.

**8** **Rim light** — A highlight on the outer edge of a surface. Rim lights are useful tools for helping an object stand out from its surroundings.

**9** **Local Color** — The color of the object itself, independent of colored light.

Where you position the main subject of your composition in relation to the primary light source defines the direction of light in the scene. The direction of light controls the size and placement of the shadows which in turn influences what parts of a subject gets emphasized and what subdued.

Lighting from the side, for example, will create a distinct lit side and a distinct shadow side in a subject. This increases contrast and generally brings out the subject's dimensionality and textures. Conversely, lighting the same subject from the front will flatten out the form, lose texture and reduce depth by providing a relatively even toned light across the frame.

Directing the light to come from behind a subject, or other angles which cause a lot of what the camera sees to be lost in shadow, can also make for powerful visuals. Here, the subject is reduced to a silhouette or rim-lit shape which, depending on the context and other design elements, can make the subject look either beautiful and poetic or mysterious and threatening.

One can also experiment with reversing normal perception by lighting the subject from an unusual direction such as from below. This can have a disconcerting effect on the viewer, as something seemingly familiar appears drastically different from what they are used to seeing.

# LIGHTING
## SETUPS

Kinds of lights used to describe a lighting setup:

**Key Light** — The main light that illuminates the object. It defines the 'direction' of the lighting and often is rooted in found elements inside the scene, such as a window or lamp.

**Fill Light** — Less intense than the key light, the fill light illuminates the shadow side of an object making the shadows more transparent.

**Back Light** — Light placed behind an object to set it off from the background.

**Kicker** — A smaller light than the others, it is used to punch up a minor area of the character or frame, such as a detail in the hair or room.

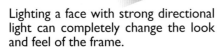

Lighting a face with strong directional light can completely change the look and feel of the frame.

Harsh side-lighting can make the shot more compelling and dramatic by using diagonals.

Uplighting in a very high key can be a bit disconcerting as it presents the face in a completely new viewpoint.

Backlighting where only a rim is used to suggest the figure can make a character mysterious or threatening.

Lighting a face solely from both sides leaves a shadow area only in all major frontal planes of the face, creating a very unusual pattern of light and shade.

Top lighting creates pockets of shadows under the eyes and nose and can be mysterious as well as beautiful depending on the harshness of the light.

The important factor to keep in mind when working with direction is to have a result oriented approach. Experiment until you feel your visual is reflecting your desired intent. Sometimes you can have very unusual setups which break all the rules for what would traditionally be considered the 'ideal' lighting for a scene.

Don't focus on generic terms like top lighting, back lighting, and so on. What these represent in the mind of a beginner is usually so limited that it does more harm than good. The best way to learn is to actually create a lighting setup and experiment hands on. This doesn't have to be complicated or expensive. You can start even by just moving your table light around an apple! The important thing is to pay attention to the effects of your moving the light around. What is happening visually, what is going on emotionally?

Most scenes usually have more than one light source. These need to relate to each other and be positioned and directed around the subject in a way which combined gives the desired effect. Here are some examples of light placements used to enhance certain aspects of a scene and create mood in a composition.

## 3-point lighting hollywood/glamour light

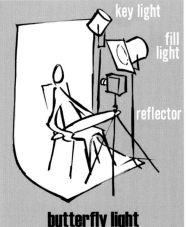

## butterfly light

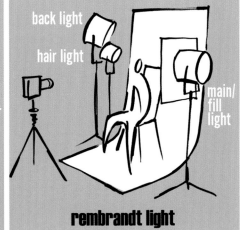

## rembrandt light

This is a fundamental three light standard setup used in film and video. The main light, or key light, is placed to the front and one side of the subject and used as the main source of illumination for the player. This positioning creates shadows and gives dimensionality to the face of the player. The shadow side of the face is lit by the fill light, used to control the transparency of the shadows. The stronger the fill light, the more transparent the shadows. Finally, a back light is used to create a rim on one side of the player really setting it and separating it from the background.

Butterfly lighting consists of lighting a face from above and in front, angled downward and aligned with the frontal view of a player. A reflector placed below and in front of the player is often used to reduce the shadows under the eyes while still retaining a degree of flattering definition in the features. Very effective for emphasizing beauty and a sharp elegance, it especially compliments a subject with high cheekbones and slender features. Getting its name from the butterfly-like shadow produced under the nose, this is a common lighting setup used especially in glamour portrait photography for women.

Named after the famous Dutch painter who commonly used this setup to light his powerful portraits, Rembrandt lighting consists of lighting a face with two lights or a light and a reflector placed high on either side of the subject angled in. This produces a pattern of *chiaroscuro*, or light and dark, on the face, such that there is a distinctive triangle of light underneath the eye on the shaded side of the face. This kind of lighting is very effective for creating moody and atmospheric portraits high in drama.

# LIGHTING
# SETUPS

The use of lighting setups to control mood is by no means limited to just the human face. The principles discussed in the previous pages can be just as effective with props or establishing shots.

In a composition where the focal point is not a character, the key is to think of one object in the frame as the 'character' element. This can be anything in the location: a chair, a tree or a house. Now, this object can be treated in the same way as we did with the human face. How much of the object do you want to reveal and how much shroud in darkness? How much do you want to distort the regular appearance of this object by lighting? Which of the different lighting setups allows for the most appealing patterns in the light and shadow elements? Here are examples of how these ideas can be applied to a simple house.

# Here are examples of how these ideas can be applied to a simple house

Similar to the face, lighting from the side brings out the dimensionality of an object. When contrast is high, this can make for a dramatic play of light and shadow in the frame and the dimensionality adds tension.

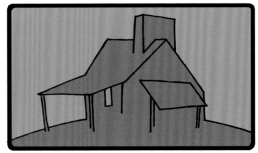

With a diffused light source that throws a soft light everywhere, no shadows are created. This can be effective for quiet and poetic scenes. Be careful to ensure the other design elements in the frame compensate by adding visual interest or the shot might become too dull.

Side lighting when the light is softer allows for the pattern of light and shadow without making things overly dramatic. This can result in scenes that can be visually beautiful as they somewhat bring out the dimensions of an object without over-emphasizing them.

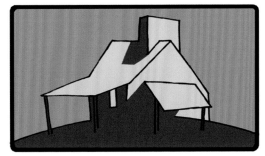

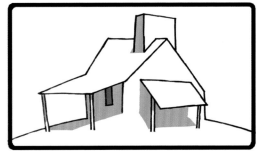

Side lighting with softer light in a high key setup can make for an upbeat scene. This is good for a neutral or comedic scene.

Back lighting, as with the face, completely obscures an object in darkness making it seem ominous. It can also be a useful tool when you want to emphasize the silhouette of an object.

Back lighting combined with a small accent light can make for incredibly dramatic and powerful scenes. Covering most of the object in dark and just lighting a small part can be a great way to evoke beauty or mystery.

149

# BRIGHTNESS

Brightness or intensity of light refers to the strength and quantity of light in a scene. A low key scene is one with an overall low level of brightness and little illumination, such as the medium shot of a character carrying a candle through a dark hall. A high key scene is one which is overall quite bright or well illuminated, such as the exterior shot of a landscape on a sunny day. Besides being a necessary tool for seeing, the amount of illumination in a scene is one of the most significant aspects of light for setting the mood.

Low key, or dim lighting, uses the darker half of the value scale to create compositions and tends to make for moody, atmospheric images. Night scenes, dim lit interiors and dramatic moments are usually handled with low key lighting. We are conditioned to be afraid of the dark and low key lighting capitalizes on this psychological tendency to induce a 'darker', more serious or threatening feel to the visual. Low key compositions can also be exceedingly beautiful. A composition made of silhouettes, for example, often makes for poetic images through its reduction in detail. The few lights in such a shot seemingly glow with intensity as they contrast so greatly with the rest of the image.

  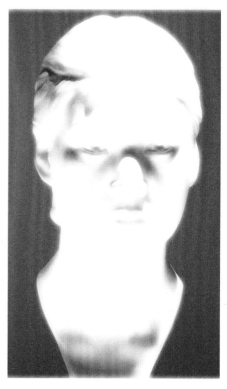

The only thing that varies in these three shots is the overall brightness of the scene. The first shot is relatively medium key in nature with transparent shadows used primarily to model the form. Scenes with this level of brightness are generally used for neutral interactions or dialogue.

In the middle is the same shot under-exposed to a lower key. Notice how the mood of the shot immediately drops to become more dramatic and tense. Details in such compositions are often deliberately lost in dark cast shadows and unlit areas, adding a sense of mystery.

The last one in the row is an over-exposed scene in a very high key. There is a loss of detail in this image as well, but with a completely different emotional impact from the previous one. Though exaggerated in this example, very high key lighting can be extremely effective to showcase purity, beauty or divinity.

When working with low key images, be sure to not lose the focal point entirely in the interest of mood. Use the few lights in your composition in service of your centre of interest and create the maximum area of contrast around it. Large amounts of darks in a low key composition can be used to unify the colors and composition, and provide a tremendous sense of moodiness to the image.

Conversely, high key or brightly lit scenes tend to use the lighter half of the value scale or all of it. These scenes can be used to depict a state of normalcy in the world of the story and are very effective for light-hearted or comedic moments. The presence of light is considered to be a purifying force, associated with white and daytime and an abundance of it is usually a source of comfort for the viewer.

Carefully control the number of shapes and colors present in the high key scene. Since most things receive a good deal of light, every color, shape and texture is very visible and consequently demands attention. It is very easy for the composition to end up feeling cluttered, or for the viewer's eye to get overwhelmed and distracted from the focal point. Eliminate unnecessary elements in the scene altogether and carefully position what remains to lead the eye to the focal point.

# QUALITY

Quality of light describes the nature of illumination in a scene. One directional, concentrated or direct lighting results in what is called hard light, while multi-directional, diffused or indirect lighting is soft light. The quality of light affects the contrast, shadows, and mood in a scene.

Spotlights, headlights, midday sunlight, or any other point source lighting usually results in hard lighting. A subject lit by hard light will generally produce stark contrasts, dark and sharp cast shadows, and clearly delineated lit sides and shaded sides. This kind of lighting makes for vibrant colors, amplified textures and a general increase in the contrast within a scene. Hard lighting can be very effective for strong dramatic compositions, showcasing the planes or dimensions of an object and emphasizing the harsher side of a scene.

When working with hard light, it is important to use the cast shadows and highlights as strong design elements within the composition. Ensure that no cast shadow is accidentally placed or creating an undesirable shape on the subject. Since you are working with strong contrasts, pay special attention to balancing and unifying the image.

On the other hand, light from overcast days, sunsets, sunrises, fog and cast through other material like cloth makes for soft lighting. Soft lighting is created by diffusion of light rays causing them to illuminate the scenes from several directions at once. This results in gentle, if any, cast shadows with soft edges and gradual gradients. These scenes are most effective for compositions requiring subtle variations in tone and color, emphasizing smoothness or soft-ness in a subject, and dealing with sensitive or subdued story points.

Soft lighting can produce stunning compositions. When working with soft light, interplay the gradients of your scene to alternate light on dark and dark on light. Ensure you create a distinct focal point despite the subtle variations in tone and color. Position your soft lights in such a way that the subject retains some dimension despite the all-over lighting.

When designing a shot and picking a light source, consider how the quality of light will affect the mood. What visual and emotional aspects of the subject would this be used to bring out? Choose the weather conditions, times of day and other aspects of the scene to fit the kind of light you have decided to use.

# SOURCE

The source of light chosen to illuminate a scene has a definite impact on the look and feel of the frame. Take, for example, a medium shot of a man and a woman facing each other. Picture this exact same setup being lit in turn by an overcast sky, a candle and a neon sign. Each scene would look and feel completely different.

Every type of source carries its own unique visual and emotional connotations. Capitalizing on these for storytelling purposes requires two things: a thorough visual understanding of what exactly light from various sources looks like, so it can be accurately simulated in your medium. And the emotional sensitivity to pick from all choices available the one that is functional as well as most appropriate for the story moment.

Keep a look out for how different light sources affect the look and feel of the world around you. How does your neighborhood look and feel on a sunny day? How about on an overcast day? How does it feel at night with artificial lights? What kind of scenes do you think each of these would be appropriate for? Do the same for people. How does someone you know look in an office with fluorescent lighting? What about when lit by a warm lamp? What aspects of his or her character is emphasized with each of these? Constantly milking the light in your environment for potential will sharpen your perception to ideas as well as opportunities.

Beyond the mood, the choice of light sources also affects focal points in a scene. Using a solitary lamp or a candle, for example, unifies the shapes in a composition since it spotlights only a small area, throwing the rest of the scene around into darkness. Completely the opposite occurs when you use a diffused light source like floodlights or an overcast sky.

Don't always go for the obvious solution. It is amazing how being present and open to experimentation and trying out a hunch can often result in far more interesting and successful visuals than the stereotypical stock approach. Intuition will be a product of time and experience. Play with photographing various subjects under the influence of different kinds of light sources and make notes regarding your observations. Keep in mind that your knowledge will really be tested by the additional challenge of being restricted to only picking from sources available in the scope of the script.

Ultimately, the greater your mental archive and understanding of the hundreds of light sources out there, the better your chances of coming up with a masterstroke which is the perfect blend between visual, practical and emotional requirements for a shot.

Shadows are as integral a part of any lighting setup as light itself. It is the balancing element in the frame without which the lit areas would really have no significance. There are two major types of shadows: attached shadows and cast shadows.

Attached shadows, which form on the object itself, have been touched upon in the sections on quality and brightness. To recount, the major thing to observe here is the rate of fall-off and the transparency of the shadow area. Heavier and more serious scenes tend to have a sharp or quick fall-off and usually have the shadows being very opaque. This often works well for scenes depicting violence or a horror motif. Less dramatic scenes would have a slower fall-off rate. Often, shadows here would be extremely transparent, their only purpose being to give volume to the forms. Attached shadows are of course also largely dependent on the nature of the form itself. Smooth objects like spheres will have slow fall-offs, but cubes would have a sharp break between the light and shadow side even with soft light.

Cast shadows involve the shadow thrown by one object onto the surface of another. Using cast shadows creatively offers endless compositional possibilities for visual storytelling. For example, showing an action like a man being stabbed through its cast shadow rather than the actual action in all its explicit detail. This makes for a much more visually interesting choice and also often increases rather than lessens the drama and effectiveness of the scene as it leaves

something to the imagination. As this also somewhat obscures the action, it adds an air of tension to the frame. Cast shadows generally serve to heighten the sense of mystery or drama in a scene. Certain genres like film noir made cast shadows one of the signature elements, but this by no means has to be restricted to scenes that only aim to provoke fear.

Creative use of cast shadows can also open a whole range of visual possibilities generating powerful visual subtext. For example, the cast shadow of a large man falling on a child makes a strong statement about the child facing trouble ahead. This has no actual rationale. For all we know, the man could be a loving father. However, in the visual world your film inhabits, this makes complete sense.

Finally, cast shadows are also very useful as design elements. They can serve as directional lines in a composition and help lead the eye; create depth by traveling in the z plane or being a repeating element; and, most importantly, simplify the scene into large major shapes by combining several objects broadly into lit areas and shadow areas.

Pay as much attention to how you place the shadows in a scene as you do to how you design the light. The examples above and alongside are just the tip of the iceberg. There are literally hundreds of ways you can use shadows to further expression. Study films, photographs and illustrations and notice how these have been used by storytellers of the past. Soon you will start to see ways you can do so in the future.

# WORKING WITH LIGHT

Now that you are familiar with several basic concepts of lighting, let's organize this knowledge into a cohesive and usable structure to effectively design the light in a shot. This will deal with the visual design aspect of film lighting applicable to all mediums rather than technicalities regarding using studio lights or digital lighting software.

Begin by identifying the essential aspects of a story moment which needs to be represented in a scene. These consist of basics like the scene being an interior or an exterior, time of day, any light continuity requirement from a previous shot, color script guidelines, weather conditions and even potential light sources mentioned in the script. For example, 'he slowly moved through the dark room with a flashlight'. These are the instructions or limitations which the rest of your lighting scheme will have to work around. In the absence of specific descriptions for these in the script, think of the story point in your scene and fill in these blanks with what you feel would be most appropriate. For example, a dramatic scene might work better at night than during the day.

Next, consider the emotional requirements and intensity of the scene. Does it deal with dramatic and intense emotions, or soft and subtle ones? Sometimes just the process of describing the emotional pace of a scene can be indicative of certain lighting decisions. For example, a 'subdued' scene suggests the use of softer cooler colored light. This 'subtext' in the scene is a dimension which can be most effectively des-cribed by the masterful use of light.

Considering all the information you gathered from the above two steps, let's start making some decisions. First, how much light should this scene have? Broadly speaking, do you think this scene will be most effective as a low key scene dealing with a large area of dark with spots of light here and there or a high key scene where a majority of the scene is in light with areas of shadow here and there? Think back to our discussion regarding how this quantity of light will impact the emotional fabric of the shot. This first decision will affect a lot of your succeeding choices.

Next, consider if you want to achieve this quantity of light from several sources or from just one. Again, be mindful of the requirements of the script or location when choosing these. Would this shot work better in the gentle tones and gradual transitions of a soft, diffused light or dramatic shadows and strong contrasts of a hard, point source light? What degree of softness or hardness would be appropriate?

In the case of a hard light, the next factor of light direction becomes even more crucial. How do you want to orient your primary light source to the principal subject in your scene? Be mindful of how different light directions will emphasize different aspects of your subject. Do you want to bring out the subject's textures and dimensions using side lighting? De-emphasize form using flat lighting? Or use an unusual lighting angle to make the scene more dramatic? Be very conscious of where the shadows of a scene will fall as you move the light around.

Having done this, consider the intensity of your fill or reflected light. Would this scene work best with shadows which are completely opaque or quite transparent? What about the color of the shadows? The degree of contrast between the lit side and the shadow side of the frame will have a powerful impact on the mood of a scene.

Having thus blocked out the major lighting decisions of your scene, stand back and review it. Is it working? Perhaps the fill light needs to be stronger? Would the shot work better if you moved the key light a little more to the side? Fine tune your image and make any modifications to earlier decisions you feel necessary. Ultimately, the visual needs to work.

At this point you should also scan the scene for any additional requirements. Perhaps the subject could use a backlight to distinguish it a bit more from the background? Maybe you want to punch up one area of the frame and tone down another? Each lighting setup has to be approached as its own entity. Constantly analyze if the intent of one of your lighting decisions is coming through, rather than relying on formulaic approaches to achieve emotional effects.

Keep in mind this is just one introductory way of approaching lighting. Ultimately, you will develop an intuitive understanding of all these parts and just 'know' what a scene needs. Before that time, however, it is important to think consciously about each dimension of light and use every tool you have to make a powerful visual statement.

A

NEXT

# CAMERA

Whether you are working with CG, live action, or traditional animation, the point at which you start to think in terms of the camera is when your idea starts to become a visual story.

So far, what we have discussed in light and color can be considered the window dressing of a shot. Compare this with designing a font to intensify the visual impact of a piece of text. In that case, the camera would represent the actual text and what it says. The mood in the shot on the left might be coming from several elements in the frame, but the basic story point to be communicated, ie 'on an island in the middle of a lake was a monastery and a few houses surrounding it' is read that way due to the positioning of the camera. While the other elements are, in a way, more a supporting cast meant to enhance, the camera represents the primary communication tool responsible for delivering the basic meat and veggies of the script.

One often hears of terrific works of fiction that were completely destroyed by a terrible translation into a different language. Unfortunately, this is too often true in the case of film. No matter how good your script and how perfect the sets and performances, the audience will ultimately only experience those aspects of your film that survive being translated through the eyes of your camera. This is, therefore, probably the most important part of visual storytelling.

All your decisions regarding camera setup, such as how far the camera is away from the subjects, its height, the angle it makes, point of focus, depth of field, choice of lens, and movement will define how we read the shot — as well as how we feel about it. This section focuses on exploring these tools and understanding how to use them to achieve your narrative goals.

# PERCEIVING CAMERA

The best way to sharpen your perception of the camera is to turn off the sound and analyze sequences from films you have already seen. For film analysis to be effective, it is crucial that your mind focuses on study rather than entertainment. The reason it's important to analyze films you have already seen is that all good cinematography is motivated by story. In order for you to understand the decisions regarding why the camera was used a particular way, you have to know what this was.

Do quick and loose thumbnails as a tool to deepen your perception of the frame. These do not have to be pretty. Their purpose is merely to make you notice more and be a shorthand for storing ideas.

When studying a sequence, ask yourself why a cinematographer made those particular choices: What is the format used and why? How would it have affected the feel if a different format had been used? What are the various types of shots in the sequence? Why was an event depicted using a close up, while another one is portrayed by a medium shot? Is the depth of field deep or shallow? Do you think this was an artistic choice or one resulting from the limitations of the set? How would this shot have looked if the depth of field had been different? What about our point of view? Is the camera lower or higher than the players? When studying the camera, it is as important to analyze a sequence in motion as it is in freeze frame. Does the camera move during the sequence? At what point? What was the reason for this camera movement? Is the movement smooth and gentle or erratic and shaky? How does this affect the shot?

Constantly asking yourself questions like these when watching films will change you from a passive consumer to an active student of cinema. You will start to learn from everything from commercials to feature films. If some of this seems confusing or overwhelming, it will only be for a short time. The more you watch things with this questioning approach in mind, the clearer and more intuitive the concepts will become. Eventually, analysis will become so second nature to you that you will do it without even trying.

Bear in mind that it is better to thoroughly analyze just a small commercial or one sequence from a film rather than casually look at the camera work for hours. You are doing these exercises to learn and the quality of your study is as important as the quantity. Focus on understanding each aspect of the camera work for a film piece by piece. Take a small chunk at a time, and within that choose to focus on just one thing such as camera movement, or types of shots. A separate sequence and aspect of camera can be tackled at another time.

# IMPROVISATION

Over the next few pages, we are going to discuss several approaches and principles that can be applied towards creating good camera work for a story. Before examining the theories involved, let's take a few minutes to ground ourselves in how organic this process is in reality.

Creating the look of a film rarely occurs in a series of perfectly linear and structured steps. More often than not it involves a lot of searching, trial and error, building on ideas, working with circumstances and, in all probability, a good deal of fighting the windmills. Several people with different priorities and diverse areas of expertise have to work together to realize the vision of a director, and do so within a particular time and budget. With so many variables thrown in the mix, only in a handful of cases do we find an idea ending up being shot exactly as it was envisioned on day one. Fully accepting and embracing the mercurial nature of this process lies at the heart of successfully operating in a real world production.

Once you begin to understand the language of a camera, you will doubtless come up with many ideas you want to try while visualizing each story. It is important to realize that these thoughts conceived at the initial stages of a production should be considered merely as first points of departure rather than a final word on the subject. At most beginnings, information is too slight and directions too vague to make any concrete decisions or calculated choices. No matter how perfect an idea may seem, some circumstances further down the road may force you to change it. Often some of the best decisions are born out of such necessity! The monumental film *Apocalypse Now* has a scene at the end where the audience

gets to meet, for the first time, Walter Kurtz, an infamous general who has been built up the entire length of the movie. The production found itself facing a major problem towards the end of shooting when Marlon Brando, who plays Kurtz, showed up on set grossly overweight. Forced to abandon whatever plans he originally had for the scene, director Francis Ford Coppola shot an improvised version where he attempted to fix this by keeping Brando hidden in darkness for almost the entire length of the sequence. Today, this choice is credited towards making the scene one of the most powerful in cinema history.

It's important to understand the basic concepts, have a sense of direction and push for what you want, but recognize when something needs to be reconsidered. An overly rigid approach to filmmaking will result in a lot of frustration for you as well as your crew. Learning to recognize better opportunities and thinking up ways to incorporate your old ideas into new circumstances is as important a skill as learning to come up with ideas from scratch. In a manner of speaking, the process is similar to the workings of a jazz ensemble. Everyone is constantly improvising and responding to each other, as well as the situation, creating the music bit by bit as they go along.

Even once you feel you have a good handle on all the concepts discussed in the rest of this chapter, resist the urge to come up with a fully defined and perfected plan for how you will use your camera on day one. As your project goes through various stages of production, a variety of forces, ranging from an improvement suggested in one area to budgetary limitations forcing a change in another, will modify and shape your initial concepts into being more specific to your story as well as to your team's capabilities. It is this collaboration with the other departments and changes you may have to make along the way that will ultimately give your film and filmmaking process a richness in flavor.

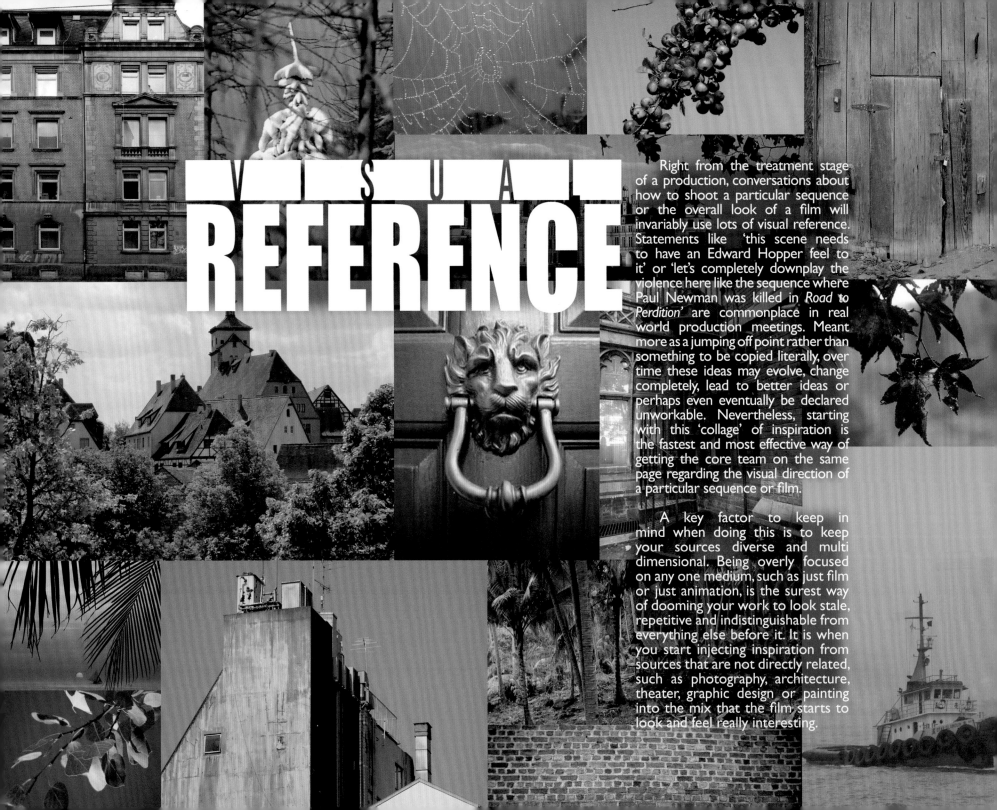

# VISUAL REFERENCE

Right from the treatment stage of a production, conversations about how to shoot a particular sequence or the overall look of a film will invariably use lots of visual reference. Statements like 'this scene needs to have an Edward Hopper feel to it' or 'let's completely downplay the violence here like the sequence where Paul Newman was killed in *Road to Perdition*' are commonplace in real world production meetings. Meant more as a jumping off point rather than something to be copied literally, over time these ideas may evolve, change completely, lead to better ideas or perhaps even eventually be declared unworkable. Nevertheless, starting with this 'collage' of inspiration is the fastest and most effective way of getting the core team on the same page regarding the visual direction of a particular sequence or film.

A key factor to keep in mind when doing this is to keep your sources diverse and multi dimensional. Being overly focused on any one medium, such as just film or just animation, is the surest way of dooming your work to look stale, repetitive and indistinguishable from everything else before it. It is when you start injecting inspiration from sources that are not directly related, such as photography, architecture, theater, graphic design or painting into the mix that the film starts to look and feel really interesting.

This, of course, necessitates a vast knowledge of what is out there. You can't really offer much input on the technical challenges or artistic merit in creating an Edward Hopper-like atmosphere if you are not familiar with who he is and what his work is characterized by. As a visual storyteller, your appetite for the arts in general and visual arts in particular should be insatiable and fed constantly. You need to be familiar with the history of art in various relevant mediums, but also in the loop about what is happening in the contemporary scene. You need to have a deep reservoir of knowledge regarding top directors, cinematographers, photographers, painters and more and a keen under-standing of the components that make up their visual style. Most of all, you need to have a tremendous archive of visual imagery across media and time that the director can tap into while putting across what he or she is trying to communicate.

At the beginning of a production, an inspiration board is a useful tool for achieving this shared aesthetic. This simply involves gathering all forms of visual inspiration for a particular scene or aspect of the style in one spot accessible to the crew for quick reference. A soft board containing several Caravaggio prints, for example, might suffice as a lighting guide for the film until something more sophisticated is developed further into production. One can have similar guides for staging, composing, costume design, set design and more.

As the production unfolds and more and more things are locked in, the general artwork on the inspiration board can start to be replaced by pieces more specific to that production. At one stage, for example, the production designer will probably take several pieces from the lighting, architecture, costume and composition boards, combining them into a single representative concept piece depicting a specific moment in the film. Eventually all the departments will make similar artwork specific to their needs, keeping only the essence of what the director wanted from a particular piece of visual reference.

# STORYBOARD

Storyboards represent the first concrete step towards the visual translation of a script. Though this is a vast topic deserving of a whole book unto itself, a basic understanding of how storyboards fit into the larger scheme of things is essential to our discussion on cinematography.

Storyboards are essentially a series of sequential images hypothesizing the flow of shots and action for a narrative. Made during the pre-production of a film, a storyboard artist, in conjunction with the director and cinematographer, will sketch out a shot by shot version of how a scene could play out. This is then evaluated and refined, with the whole process being repeated as many times as required before the visuals work the way they need to. A relatively cheap and fast process, storyboards basically provide filmmakers with a chance to make rough drafts of their movies before committing.

Once finalized, storyboards start to serve as the blueprint of a scene. Each department scrutinizes the shots to see what is required from their side for a particular sequence. What sets need to be built? How much of it needs to built? How many shots need to be covered on a particular day of shooting? Does this shot have to match and be cut into anything later? Questions like these and more are answered, at least at the beginning, using the information presented in the storyboards. This is what serves as the basis for estimates and schedules, ultimately resulting in a budget.

Finally, storyboards also serve as a channel of communication between the various departments during production. A director can use the storyboard for a variety of functions ranging from deciding the plan of action for a particular day to communicating with his actors and crew regarding what he wants to achieve in a particular shot. In some mediums such as animation, the storyboards even serve as a jumping off point for the poses and performances of the characters.

Whether you choose to do your own storyboards as Ridley Scott once did, or prefer the Alfred Hitchcock approach of working with another artist, the tremendous value of this tool simply cannot be overstated. Used with mastery, storyboards can make for better films as well as far more efficient filmmaking processes. It would be well worth the time of anyone interested in cinematography to spend a good deal of time studying this skill.

# SHOOTING
# STYLES

Before getting into the specifics of handling individual elements of a camera setup, we should touch upon the concept of an overall shooting style.

A shooting style refers to a loose set of guidelines, established at the outset, regarding various aspects of a film's visual fabric. These could include types of lenses used, amount and nature of camera movement, duration of shots, and so on. Combined with other aspects of production design, such as lighting choices and types of sets used, these generate a visual approach for each production that is custom-fitted for the needs and limitations of that particular project. Your choice of shooting style can make, break or completely transform the way your film is experienced.

*The Blair Witch Project,* for example, was a horror film shot entirely using handheld camera/home video footage. Besides increasing the believability of the scenes and complementing the story perfectly, the shaky camera combined with ambiguous visuals added a great deal of tension to the frames. This dramatically increased the effectiveness of the film and also reduced costs of production.

Over the history of film and television, various such shooting conventions have developed for specific projects as well as across genres. Film noir, for example, is famous for having lots of tight framing and sparse images with large parts of the frame lost in darkness. As is often the case with shooting styles, the primary reason for this had more to do with commerce and technology than with aesthetics. The filmmakers simply couldn't afford to make and light large elaborate sets, so found a way to tell stories effectively without them.

It's important for visual storytellers to have a huge archive and understanding of various shooting styles. Besides being fascinating reservoirs of ideas and inspiration, several shooting conventions generate strong associations and expectations in the minds of the audience. Once understood, these can be used or subverted to achieve our narrative goals. A BBC television series by the name of *Twenty Twelve*, for example, is a witty mockumentary about a fictional committee organising the summer Olympics. All the shot choices, types of framing, camera movement and so on used in the show completely replicates what the audience would usually see in an actual documentary. This results in everything becoming much funnier as all these hilarious things keep happening in what subconsciously feels like an unscripted environment.

Be it the distinctive look and feel of '70s and '80s MTV music videos, the pointillist appoach of director David Fincher, the atmospheric cinematography of Christopher Doyle or the completely unrestricted camera seen in any of the recent visual effects heavy films, the examples and categories of conventions are endless as well as endlessly informative.

Spend some time identifying various shooting styles, as well as analyzing the ingredients that define them. Study footage from different time periods, genres, budgets, types of production, types of story and even the works of individual directors. Make notes about the kinds of formats, lenses, framing, types of shots, camera movement and choice of motifs that might be affecting an audience's experience of the story. Over the next few pages, we will look at each of these components individually and develop a deeper understanding of them.

# FORMAT

One of the first choices facing a cinematographer is what format or aspect ratio something should be shot in. This refers to the ratio between the length and breadth of a frame. There are many types of formats in film and television and each brings a different look and feel. The format you choose will have a defining impact on all compositions throughout your production and should be a carefully weighed choice balancing artistic considerations as well as practical requirements.

The first thing you need to think about is where your finished film will be seen by the viewer. Would it be on an IMAX screen, a television, an iPhone or something in between? What will be the shape of the screen? Older televisions for example were designed for the Academy Ratio (4:3) format. This meant that watching something shot in the extremely wide Super Panavision (2.35:1) meant you either had to resort to the disastrous pan-and-scan method, or be content with most of your screen covered by large black bars. While this is less of a problem nowadays with televisions being manufactured in the fairly standardized widescreen format of 16:9, who knows what the future will bring? The key point to remember is that when you are choosing how to shoot your film, you must not lose track of the primary conditions in which it will ultimately be seen.

**normal**

**3 : 4**

**widescreen**

**1 : 1.85**

**cinemascope**

**1 : 2**

**panavision**

**1 : 2.35**

Next, you need to consider the nature of your script or story. Certain stories are more about telling while others are more about showing. So is the case with various formats. Scripts involving lots of dialogue, such as a family drama, can be extremely effectively told in the old TV (4:3) ratio. Close ups are more intimate in this format and a face can be framed with ease to fill the screen. Overall, this is more effective for a relatively literal approach to visual storytelling. On the other hand, a tale of epic proportions containing several visual spectacles and told with an atmospheric flair should absolutely make use of the gorgeous anamorphic widescreen (2.35:1) format. Wider ratios are more pleasing to the eye as we fundamentally have a horizontally shaped field of vision.

Super wider formats try to replicate the experience of a person standing at a panoramic viewpoint such as the beach or top of a mountain where the field of vision stretches over a wide horizon. Such formats are better for stunning vistas and the visual poetry of each scene rather than a factual depiction of events. If your film is meant to be a visual feast, where the viewer is immersed into a stunning world, then this is the way to go.

Budget is another consideration when choosing your format. While use of specific camera equipment and lenses required to shoot super wide would be outside the scope of this book, it is usually a safe bet to assume that shooting wider will mean your production costs go up regardless of the medium. Quite simply, wider shots contain more screen-space to fill. This means more of the set has to be designed, created, lit and so on. This is no different even for digital sets or painted backgrounds. Additionally, it is also very important to consider one's personal understanding and level of comfort with a particular format. Shooting a story in the Academy Ratio (4:3) can be a very different experience from shooting it in anamorphic widescreen (2.35:1). The

rules of composition are different for each; how and how much the camera moves dramatically changes; and even editing gets affected, as some wider shots contain a lot more information than a 4:3 shot, thus needing to stay on screen for longer to be effective. It is very important to make sure you are using a ratio you have some understanding of or budget time in your production schedule to run some tests and get to know a new format.

# MOTIF

What do you think of when you think of the Shire in *Lord of the Rings*? Lush green hills with little round doors, the sound of song and laughter coming from the Green Dragon, Bilbo's house with a cozy fire? But logically speaking, the Shire probably has some barren parts, a cemetery or two, and days when it is pouring with rain as well. We just don't think of that because our perception of the Shire has been masterfully crafted using iconic visuals that fit the *idea* of the Shire. These are called motifs.

In large part, the personality of the character or location comes from the piece of it you choose to showcase. A great place to study choice of motif is theater and set design. Due to the economy of real estate on a stage, the art directors have to really distill locations into a handful of props and objects that together create an atmosphere and sense of place. Ask yourself what the most important quality of this location is from the story's perspective and try and find an object or detail in the environment that can epitomize that.

The motif is used to maintain focus and consistency. It is a theme, subject or idea that is the most distinctive and recurring feature in the film. The motif is usually repeated throughout the film to emphasize the main concept. It can be as obvious as a specific shot or as subtle as a distinct color or shape that runs through the narrative tying together key parts as you can see in the images below.

Take great care to pick the right motif for your shot or sequence. The object or part of a character you choose to define a place or person with will enhance along with your lighting and camera choices. Choosing the wrong motif can mean you end up working against the current, whereas the right one can do all the work for you.

Framing makes up a large part of the 'meat and veggies' of cinematography. This involves deciding how large you want a particular object or character to be on screen, how you position it and what angle it is seen from. These decisions will define how you 'read' the information as well as emotion in a shot. This chapter introduces several concepts we will be delving into in greater detail over the next few sections.

How large you have an object or character on screen in large part decides what the shot is about. If, for example, 90 percent of the screen is covered by a landscape, then the audience will primarily be thinking about the landscape. On the other hand, if you can see nothing but the face of a character, the shot becomes about his or her expression and emotion. This topic has been expanded upon in the section on 'shot sizes', but at the outset it is important to understand that screen space has a direct relationship to the content of a scene.

The angle from which we view an object or character adds an emotional color to the shot. We can literally 'look down' upon weak and powerless characters, much like we look at a small ant on the ground. We 'look up' to characters we want to perceive as powerful and imposing, much like a large stranger might seem to a small child. This translates into up-shots and down-shots in the language of cinematography. Think of your camera as if it is a member of your audience and ask yourself, 'how do I want this person to feel about the character in this shot?' This topic has been further expanded in the section on camera angles.

Camera-tilt is another factor that has an impact on the emotional tone of a shot. Tilting the camera immediately creates a feeling of imbalance and generates a lot of visual tension in the scene. As we discussed previously in the chapter on lines, this comes from us being constantly used to a level horizon. Camera tilts can be used to create tension in even the most mundane actions and shots.

Where on the screen you choose to position an object or character has an impact on how it is perceived. For example, placing a character very near the edge of a frame generates visual tension in the frame with that edge seeming to pull the character outwards. Avoid this unless you want to draw attention to this aspect of the shot. On the other hand, dead centre framing is also not always advisable, as it generates such little tension so as to make the scene boring. Generally, using the golden rectangle or rule of thirds is a good approach to placing your central focal point in the shot.

When framing, it is also crucial to anticipate how that particular shot is going to progress. For example, one shot might start with just one character on screen, but will later have another character enter from screen left. Leaving some empty space by framing the first character with a screen right bias creates an expectation in the audience that something in the scene is yet to occur. Any kind of imbalance of this nature that creates a visual question mark generates visual tension in the frame. You can use this in the traditional way or even reverse it by leading the audience to believe something is going to happen, but then subverting that expectation. For example, in a horror film you could have a shot of your character's reflection in a mirror on one side of the frame in a very deliberate way. This will create a strong expectation in the audience that they will be seeing something. Even though you plan on showing nothing, they will remain on the edge and entirely focused on every little thing on screen and breathe a sigh of relief when you finally cut.

FRA

MING

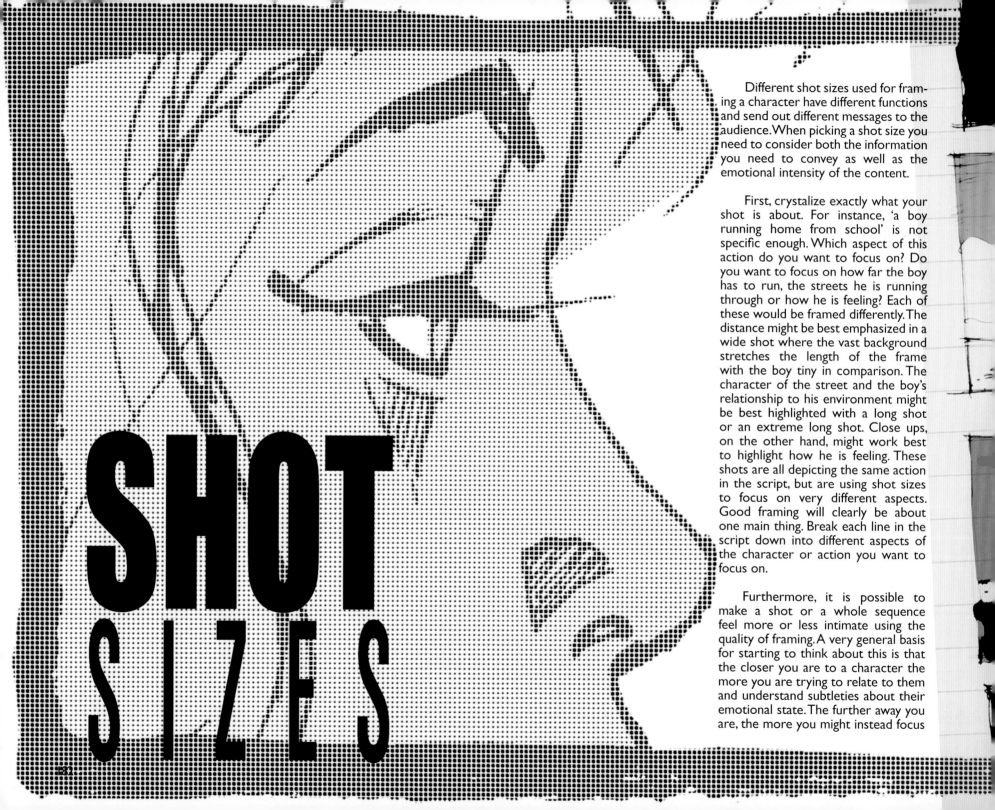

# SHOT SIZES

Different shot sizes used for framing a character have different functions and send out different messages to the audience. When picking a shot size you need to consider both the information you need to convey as well as the emotional intensity of the content.

First, crystalize exactly what your shot is about. For instance, 'a boy running home from school' is not specific enough. Which aspect of this action do you want to focus on? Do you want to focus on how far the boy has to run, the streets he is running through or how he is feeling? Each of these would be framed differently. The distance might be best emphasized in a wide shot where the vast background stretches the length of the frame with the boy tiny in comparison. The character of the street and the boy's relationship to his environment might be best highlighted with a long shot or an extreme long shot. Close ups, on the other hand, might work best to highlight how he is feeling. These shots are all depicting the same action in the script, but are using shot sizes to focus on very different aspects. Good framing will clearly be about one main thing. Break each line in the script down into different aspects of the character or action you want to focus on.

Furthermore, it is possible to make a shot or a whole sequence feel more or less intimate using the quality of framing. A very general basis for starting to think about this is that the closer you are to a character the more you are trying to relate to them and understand subtleties about their emotional state. The further away you are, the more you might instead focus

on broader qualities and actions. For example, a shot about two people taking their wedding vows might be shot using over the shoulder close ups to focus on the warm expressions of the bride and the groom. In a scenario where the same wedding was to be a cold and ceremonial affair, the majority of the scene might instead be shot with more distant and aloof framing.

Close ups tend to be very powerful because they fill the entire frame with a character or object, increasing the overall amount of movement and 'active' parts of the screen, so audience involvement is increased. Inviting audience involvement using proximity is not always a good thing though. Certain violent actions or sad moments, even though emotionally intense, can often be more powerful if implied using a wider distant framing than explicitly shown.

It is important for collaborators in other parts of the filmmaking process to be mindful of your shot sizes. Actors, for example, need to limit the amount and scale of movement for close up shots. The close up amplifies even the most subtle eye movements. Engaging in broad theatrical acting shots in close up might come across as fake over-acting. Editors need to consider how much visual information is in a shot when choosing how long a shot should stay on screen. A wide establishing shot would usually take more time to take in fully than a close up. Editors can also 'prioritize' certain characters in a dialogue sequence between characters by keeping his or her framing tighter than the other's over the course of the sequence.

183

THOUGH ULTIMATELY A MATTER OF ARTISTIC JUDGEMENT AND DEVELOPING A CUSTOMIZED LANGUAGE REGARDING FRAMING RULES FOR A FILM, IT IS USEFUL TO BE MINDFUL OF THESE CONCEPTS AS YOU START EXPLORING DIFFERENT SHOT SIZES. HERE IS AN OVERVIEW OF SOME COMMONLY USED CONVENTIONS.

**Establishing Wide Shot** — Often used in the opening shots of a new location or sequence, the establishing wide shot is used to orient the viewer to the geographical layout of the environment and our character's position within it. This shot focuses almost entirely on the environment of the character, providing the information needed to keep track of where he or she is in the rest of the sequence. These shots are also very effective for establishing scale.

establishing wide shot

**Extreme Long Shot** — Extreme long shots focus on the character and the background in equal measure and can be used to show how a character relates to his or her environment. Ideal for framing simple shots such as characters walking or running, extreme shots don't push viewers to read 'into' the action.

extreme long shot

**Long Shot** — Still focusing on both character and environment, long shots start to shift the bias more towards the character. Body language of the subject is fairly visible in long shots and starts to make an impact in the mind of the viewer.

long shot

**Medium Long Shot** — A crossover between medium shots and long shots, the medium long shot continues the transition of shifting the focus from background to character.

medium long shot

scene nr.

length / length from to

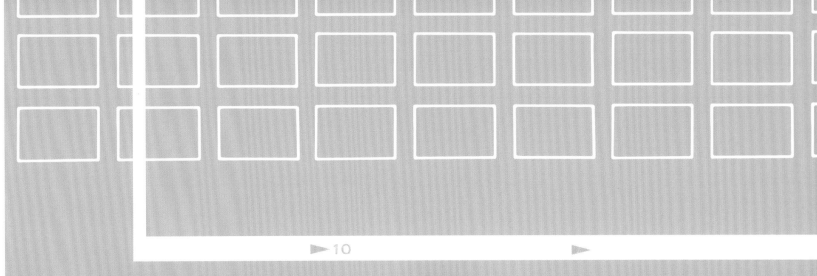

**Medium Shot** — Great for shooting two characters in one composition, posture, body language and costume are the main focuses here. While backgrounds don't command a lot of attention, a well-chosen backdrop or prop can still be used to add flavor to the frame. The face and expressions also start to gain importance in medium shots.

**Medium Close Up** — By drawing attention to the face, the focus with medium close ups starts to shift from the external to the internal world of the character. Separating the character as a clear focal point, these shots direct the undivided attention of the audience towards the subject.

**Close Up** — The viewer's attention is now completely focused on the inner world and emotional state of the character. Often making up a large section of dialogue scenes, close ups are great for revealing what's going on in a character's mind. It is crucial for actors to keep movements controlled and subtle in framing this tight and tighter.

**Big Close Up** — A stepped up version of a close up, the big close up starts to accentuate the character's thoughts and expressions even more by omitting all else from the frame. A character deep in thought can often be visually expressed by moving the camera from a close up to a big close up over the course of a shot.

**Extreme Close Up** — Very effective to show climactic character moments or heightened emotional states, extreme close ups are very useful for dramatic shots. Using an extreme close up to show a character diffusing a bomb, for example, would greatly intensify the tension of the shot with the whole frame being filled with the face and the audience focusing on the nervous eyes and beads of sweat on the forehead.

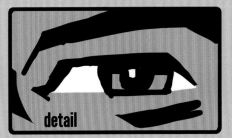

**Detail** — This refers to extremely tight framing only showcasing a small feature, such as a scar on the character or an earring in his or her ear. The detail can be used to give personality and flavor to the individual by highlighting distinctive visual chacteristics.

185

# EMOTIONAL DISTANCE

Most feature scripts contain characters that you want the audience to relate to in a variety of ways. Some, like your protagonist, you might want to make completely emotionally accessible to the viewers so that they care about him or her and feel deeply involved in his or her wins and losses. Others, such as a high status character, may be more effective if kept relatively aloof and emotionally distant. Visually controlling this emotional accessibility throughout the film plays a big part in establishing powerful character relationships and status in your narrative.

The first of the factors that affects this emotional distance between the audience and the character is, not surprisingly, physical distance. We discussed in the previous page how using a close up instead of a long shot immediately makes us much more involved in the character's emotional state. This proximity allows us to see the slightest change in the face, granting us seemingly complete access to his or her thoughts. On the other hand, an individual you can only see from a certain distance, in wide shots for example, is hard to read and retains a certain amount of mystery and status. Think of how courts in the olden days required a significant distance between the king and his subjects. This approach is very useful for portraying characters that you want the audience to perceive as hard to read, out of reach, or mythic.

This concept of distance can be further accentuated using levels of separation. Generally speaking, adding a level of separation between the camera and the character, such as a curtain, emphasizes the sense of distance between that character and the audience. Transparent or translucent divisions, heavy weather such as rain or fog, rows of people, looking through windows and doors or seeing a character through a television are some of the commonly used separators used in film. The nature of separation also affects our resulting perception. Seeing a character through prison bars, for example, sends out a very different signal from seeing him or her through a waterfall.

Distance and levels of separation can additionally be used to show some aspect of a character to character relationship within a frame. For instance, if you want to show the isolation of a particular character, keep him visually isolated in the frame by using a separator of some kind to divide the space between him or her and another character. If used appropriately and consistently, these concepts can add a tremendous sense of atmosphere and subtext to your character scenes.

Another crucial factor determining how the audience connects with a character is eye contact. The audience will generally feel uncomfortable around an individual where they don't have access to the eyes. You can capitalize on this instinct by hiding the eyes of any character that you wish to present as menacing or untrustworthy. Lighting, sunglasses, an out of focus shot or always having the character turned away from the camera are some of the ways you can obscure a character's eyes and expressions while still harnessing the power of a close up.

The last and possibly most important factor to keep in mind when controlling emotional distance for characters, is the amount of time we spend visually with that character. Human beings have a natural tendency to empathize with anything they spend a significant amount of time with. We rely on this instinct to get the audience to start caring about our protagonist. This, however, can be equally applicable to characters we don't really want the audience to start rooting for. Be cautious when dividing the amount of screen time you devote to key characters. Make sure the relative proportions reflect the priorities of who the story is primarily about. Try minimizing time spent visually focusing on anyone we do not want the audience to develop an attachment to or make sure their depiction makes them extremely emotionally inaccessible.

Whether you are using distance, separators, eye contact or amount of screen time as a way to control character to character or character to audience relationships, remember that these can and should change over time. The whole point of stories is to show characters or situations undergoing an arc that results in a change. This progression should also be reflected in your visuals. Some of the most exciting moments in film are often when we see, for the first time, a character up close after having been kept at bay emotionally and visually for a majority of the movie. The movie *Road to Perdition,* for example, starts off with us barely having access to the world of Michael Sullivan Jr. because

his son, who represents the audience's point of view, does not have access to it either. As the story progresses we see this relationship change emotionally as well as visually as we, along with Michael Sullivan Jr., are given more and more access to the world and mental state of his father. All of these little considerations when layered in can make a big overall difference to the final product.

# CAMERA
# ANGLES

Picking the right camera angle to showcase a character, action or set is crucial to a shot succeeding in its storytelling goals. This simple choice defines the way something physically appears in the frame as well as how the audience relates to it on a psychological level. Learning to control and fully use this tool gives us the ability to fill even the most mundane visual events with interest and emotion.

Let's talk about interest first. Normally we are used to seeing most things from a pretty consistent vantage point. We look up at buildings, look down on a bug and essentially look at eye level at someone walking down a street. Often changing this angle of view takes away the visual monotony of the familiar, holding our attention simply by providing a new perspective. In film, this concept can be used to charge just about any shot with visual drama. For example, a wide shot of a character walking across a desert can be made into a very arresting scene if shot with the camera perpendicular to the ground looking straight down. The dunes would make a beautiful pattern playing across the screen and the long shadow of our character gliding across the sand would provide the focal point while lending a poetic atmosphere to the image. This would provide far more visual interest than a straight wide shot taken on ground level.

When picking a camera angle for a shot, try not to always go for the obvious solution. This is usually overdone and certainly far too common to generate any visual interest. Take a few moments and visualize the action and environment in question from all 360 degrees. What possibilities does it offer? Can any of these angles be used to further the style and tone of the image as well as the requirements of the script? Is there any visually interesting feature in the environment, such as a carpet on the ground or fresco on the ceiling, that could be included to make the frame more compelling? Are there any foreground elements that can be roped in to help sell the composition or emotion? Getting into the habit of consciously making these efforts to explore beyond the first vantage point will keep your work fresh and interesting while ensuring you always have multiple options to choose from.

It is also crucial to consider the psychological impact of our choices. As mentioned in the previous paragraphs, human beings are used to seeing most things from a fairly consistent viewpoint. As with all the other visual elements of design, over time, these angles of view have come to be associated with particular types of relationships that we can use to tap into specific emotions. For example, looking up, in our human experience, usually occurs when a person or object is larger than us. This, translated by cinema into an up shot, consequently makes any object that we view from this angle seem larger and of higher status, evoking feelings of power, awe or fear. Up shots can be very successful to showcase powerful or threatening characters as well as tense and dramatic situations. The shot of a judge in a court room, for example, will probably work better if the judge is viewed in an up shot, placing him as having high status in the minds of the audience. Down shots, on the other hand, represent looking down on something and usully mean we have superiority and control over the character or object we are looking down on. This takes power away from the subject of the scene and can be very useful to showcase anything as weak, vulnerable or insignificant. A close up of a slave intending to illustrate how pathetic and helpless his condition is, for instance, would probably be a lot more effective if viewed in a down shot with the slave looking up at the camera.

As you attempt to use these associations to generate emotion in the shot, keep in mind the tremendous role of context. For example, a down shot of a character trapped in an alley way with all the right lighting and colors, will probably generate tension in the frame, but a down shot of a romantic setting with appropriate colors might not be tense at all. The same camera angles can often come to mean a variety of things depending on the situation and the other elements of film language used in the scene. It is important to not approach any of these concepts from a dogmatic perspective. Each scene is unique and each shot needs to be considered in relation to the flow of shots that come before and after it.

Keep these principles and guidelines in mind as you go about designing your shots, but feel free to play with them. Often a rule can be turned around on its head and be used in a completely new way that is just as successful. As always, there is no better way to develop an intuitive understanding of the concepts involved than by studying the masters. All great filmmakers from Orson Welles to Quentin Tarantino have their own ways of using camera angles, each of them equally valid. Regardless of how you choose to use camera angles, being aware of their capabilities and consciously attempting to get the most out of them will greatly improve the visual as well as storytelling qualities of your cinematography.

The examples here combine the concepts discussed in the last few chapters. Notice the range in visuals and moods that can be achieved for the same basic scene setup by just changing the lens and camera angle. Factors to pay special attention to are size relationships between objects, position and nature of horizon lines, how the camera is oriented to the main subject of the shot — the house in this case — which in turn controls how many sides of the subject you can see — frontal view, 3/4 view, etc. — and overall sense of space in the frame.

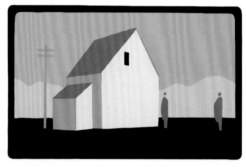

**Eye level shot with a normal lens** — This image can be thought of as our visual and emotional neutral. Perception of lines, size relationships and perspective is the same as we would see if ordinarily standing at the scene in real life.

**Down shot with a wide angle** — Proximity to the subject while using a wide angle results in distortion of planes and a fish eye effect. Notice the curved horizon and how much further the mountains feel through this lens.

**Up shot with a wide angle** — An extremely dramatic combination, the upward view combined with a wide angle lens is amplifying the perspective, size difference and sense of space in the shot. The tilted horizon, known as the Dutch tilt, also adds to the feeling of intensity and tension in the frame.

**Down shot with a normal lens** — An unusual vantage point showing multiple planes of the house adds visual interest to the scene. The normal lens results in the sense of perspective and size relationships still being fairly regular.

**Up shot with a normal lens** — The angle results in an increased sense of perspective and a more dramatic image. However, size relationships between objects do not get amplified, as would be the case with an up shot using a wide angle lens (bottom left).

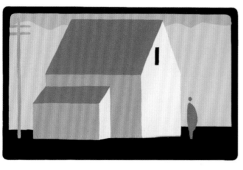

**Profile with a telephoto lens** — A very flat and boring shot. The choice of angle results in the object appearing flat and dimensionless. The parallel lines, lack of perspective and flattened distance between the house and the mountain is due to the long lens.

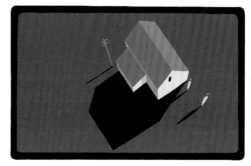

**Down shot with a telephoto lens** — Mostly a result of the unusual camera angle here, the shot is presented from a bird's eye view of the scene offering an alternative perspective and greater visual interest.

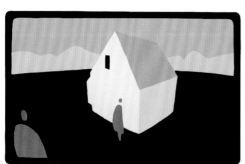

**Down shot with a wide angle** — Seeing multiple planes of the house adds visual interest without creating too much intensity. Notice the amplification in distance between the figures due to the wide angle.

**Frontal view with a telephoto lens** — A visually quiet and almost boring shot. The choice of angle offers the least amount of visual drama in the subject by showing only one plane while the long lens reduces the perspective, size difference and sense of space in the frame.

191

# CAMERA
# CONCLUSION

Cinematography is to visual story-tellers what words are to writers. Taking the time to learn and think about the language of film every time you are deciding how to say something visually will make a big difference to how the audience receives it emotionally.

Take time to study your favorite cinematographers and analyze how they use format, shot size, camera angles, lenses and distance to weave an emotional fabric that you experience through the story. Before you start your own shooting, take the time to study references, decide on shooting styles and workshop ideas through storyboards. Over time, all of these concepts will become second nature to you and you will find yourself getting fully fleshed out ideas for terrific shots in your head immediately even as you read a script for the first time.

# C O M P O

So far in the book we have discussed line, shape, color, camera and many other elements that go into making a good film frame. Mastery of each of these will go a long way towards improving your visual storytelling, but now we turn our attention to the most important skill of all. The art of combining individual parts into something that works as a whole — composition.

A well composed film frame is one that is instantly readable, visually interesting and evokes the right mood. Doing all this requires you to be a skilled craftsman who knows the elements of design, a good storyteller who comes up with interesting solutions to visual problems and a ruthless editor who is always asking if something is essential to a shot.

SITION

# visual order

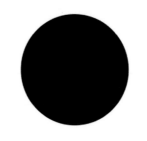 · size

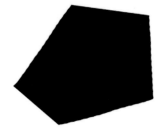

## linear/shapes ——————————

## format

## values

color

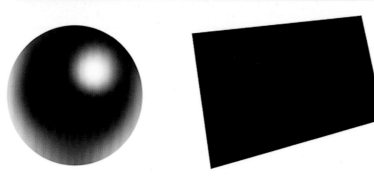

## 3-D/flat

# detail/rhythm

# G

Composition refers to the organization of elements within the frame. A GOOD composition, however, is far more than merely the sum of it's parts. A good composition is an experience!

The best compositions have three qualities. They are clear, appealing and evocative. First and foremost a good composition should be clear. It should show absolutely clearly, the information that a particular shot is supposed to communicate. This could be as simple and obvious as the boy forgot to close the door' or as subtle as, ' The boy thought of his mother.' A challenging task in itself. One has to find the right visual elements and arrange them in a way which makes this message legible in the few seconds for which this image will remain on screen. This alone however is not enough. A good composition must also be appealing. This does not necessarily mean that all our compositions should be in the strictest sense of the word, beautiful, but refers to them having some element of visual charm which makes them compelling to watch. After all, we are in the entertainment industry, our images need to hold the audience's attention!

Finally, a good composition is evocative. This refers to the power of composition to intensify our emotional experience and the involvement in the story. This process of making emotion resonate through a particular arrangement of the frame is easily the most fascinating dimension of this art and is often the quality which separates good compositions from the great one's.

Consistently coming up with good composition for film requires a thorough knowledge and understanding in two areas. Visual design and film language.

Visual Design is about the basic rules of picture making applicable to all forms of two dimensional design. It deals with concepts such as harmony, contrast, balance and rhythm and is a necessary basis for the creation of any successful image regardless of the medium. The upcoming chapters on design will explore each of the elements and principles of design in great depth, showcasing through examples how these seemingly abstract concepts relate to the creation of simple and obvious as the boy forgot to close the door' or as subtle as, ' The boy thought of his mother.' A challenging task in itself. One has to find the right visual

# information amount

# realistic/abstract

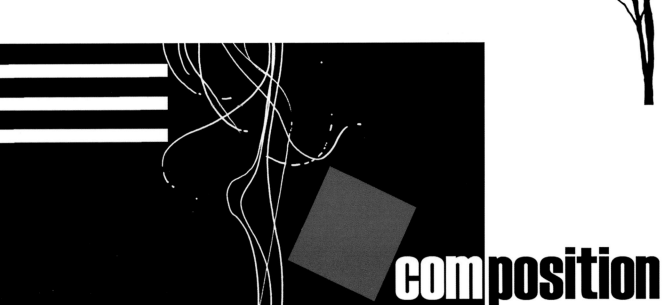

# composition

Think about the many aspects we have discussed that go into making an image. What kind of lines are used? What kind of shapes? How big or small is something? What kind of contrasts are at play? This diverse array of perspectives needs to be considered and now carefully composed into a cohesive visual order that works for the requirements of your shot.

One of the incredible things about composition is that it has much more to do with understanding and decision making than your ability to draw or paint. This is why you have artists with different degrees of drawing skills from animation to live action who have different approaches to creating stunning compositions.

To make sure we keep the conversation focused on the principles of composition rather than how to make pretty pictures, we are going to begin talking about this art using the simplest design elements possible — the basic shapes. Once you have grasped the core concept, the same principle is easily applicable to more representational film frames.

# Not WORKing!

Composition is defined as the arrangement of parts into a harmonious whole. But what exactly does that mean? Let's try to understand by first examining what a bad composition looks like.

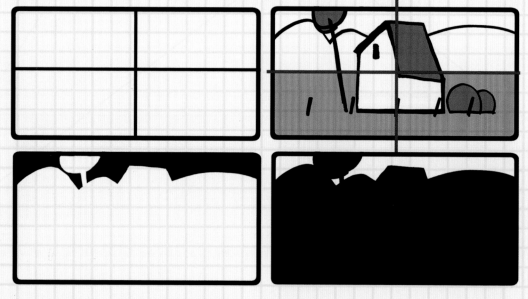

In the image on the left, notice how the distribution of space is too even and the positive and negative shapes are not particularly balanced or readable. The silhouette is not grouping the objects in any meaningful way. There isn't a clear hierarchy of focal points, and some focal points are too close to the edge of the frame. The result is your eye is pulled in every direction. This is a composition that just doesn't work.

# better

Here are some different arrangements using the same objects. Though each of these is using a different lens and a different scale, all of these are individually clear images. The positive and negative shapes are interestingly designed and help with a quick read. There is an asymmetrical division of space using the principles of golden ratio and rule of thirds, and there is a visual balance in the frame. The silhouette makes for a quick read, and the focal points have a clear hierarchy. Objects are not cropped in a confusing manner and nothing is too close to the edge of the frame.

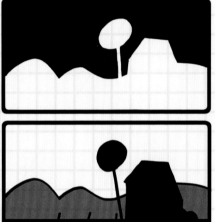

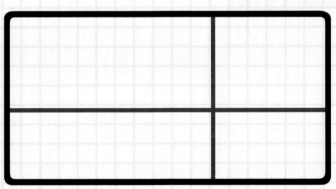

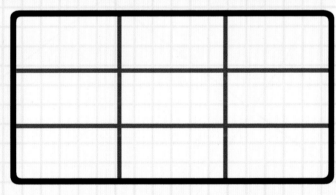

In this case, the composition is designed to help the viewer understand exactly what it is that they need to be looking at, and doing so in an instant. This makes for a better arrangement of the parts and, on the most basic level, makes for a better composition.

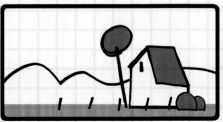

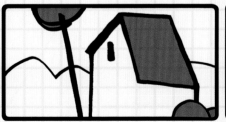

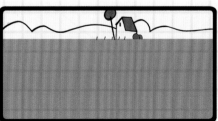

# Where to start...

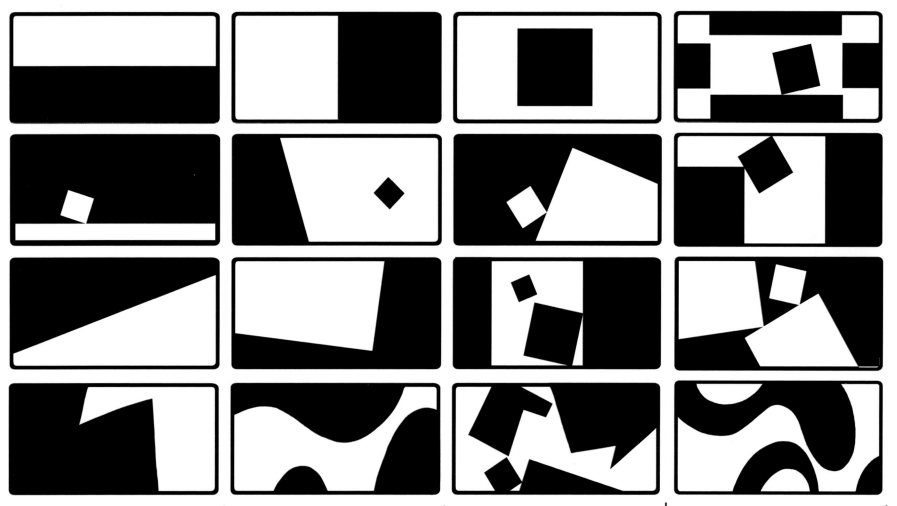

A lot of artists feel a blank page is one of the hardest things to conquer. Where does the character go? How far should the camera be? Is it going to be negative on positive or positive on negative? The result of being faced with making all these decisions, is often paralysis. You decide life would be simpler if you close your sketchbook and go get a coffee instead.

When you come back, try starting your next composition by simply dividing the space. Nothing too complicated, just splitting the frame into two parts: black and white. Notice how the frame immediately starts to take on a particular character. Experimenting with different divisions of space can be a fun and almost zen-like way to start composing an appealing image.

As you experiment, you'll notice that different divisions have a completely different feel to them. For example, the top row of compositions come across as a bit boring and unnatural — more like a graphic design then a good film composition. This is because the shapes and division are too similar and symmetrical. The lower rows have examples of more interesting and successful space divisions.

Once you have a good major split, you can start to further divide the frame by adding other shapes into the white spaces. These additional shapes should be placed with careful consideration of the negative shape they are within, because this negative shape is now your new frame. Experiment with these limited pieces until you come up with arrangements that look interesting. Congratulations, you have tricked yourself into starting compositions.

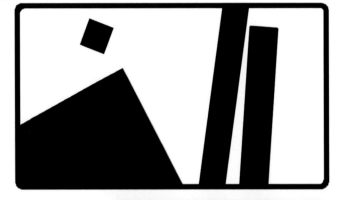

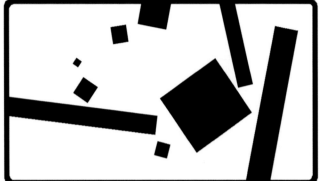

One of the most common problems found in a lot of weak compositions today is that they are overloaded with detail. The average amount of time a shot will stay on screen is just 5 to 10 seconds. For the audience to understand all the information you want to communicate to them in that time, you have to find a visual way to say whatever you are trying to say with simplicity.

When you are looking at any image, notice all the areas where your eye is drawn. If it's a good composition, these will be just one or two places in the frame. If it is not a good composition, your eye will feel pulled in several different ways without any clear order or progression.

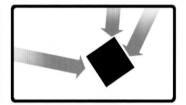

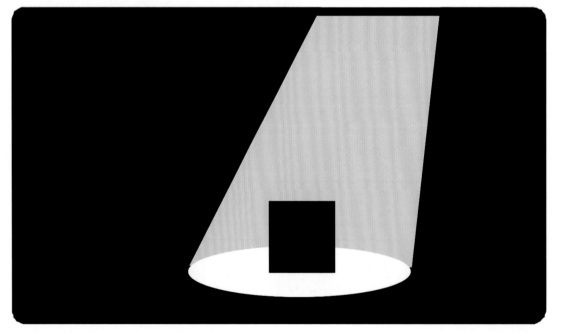

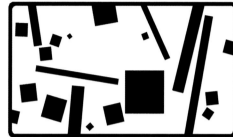

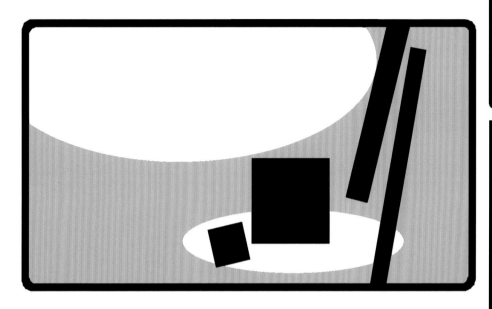

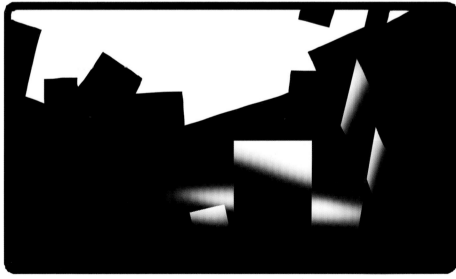

Often the nature of the scene will necessitate a lot of elements being on screen at the same time. In this case, use lighting and staging to control the focal points. Thinking of your set as a stage with the lights turned off will reduce most of the visual information you see on screen into a handful of big shapes. Now you have the equivalent of a blank canvas to start from. Use a spotlight to 'pull' a few elements back into focus while leaving the rest obscured.

Be sure to pick only a few spotlit areas per frame. It's usually better to split an idea into multiple shots rather than try and fit too many focal points within one frame. The only things that should be in the frame for any given shot are the ones that are absolutely necessary to that specific idea. Thinking of a spotlight is also a good way to control the amount of detail in the image. The areas within the spotlight can have more detail than the rest of the frame with it fading off further away from the focal point.

The focal point refers to the dominant point of interest in the picture. It is important to divide the frame into areas that require attention and areas that don't. This will allow you to define where to put the contrast in the image and where to avoid it. Not doing so results in contrasting elements scattered across the frame which, in turn, results in the viewer's attention being scattered across the frame as well. This result, as can be seen in the first thumbnail on the right, is chaos.

Compare this to the next few thumbnails in the same row where similar elements have been organized in different ways to create very clear and defined focal points. The contrast in this case is focused to a specific area in the frame and the rest of the frame becomes a supporting cast. Shapes similar to the 'hero' shape are

removed, so that this shape stands out. A large number of elements are grouped together by proximity so they are seen as just one or two elements. Everything is made darker so that the focal point, which is light, can shine. Such shots with clearly defined focal points are much easier and quicker to understand.

According to Chinese philosophy, *yin* and *yang* represent the idea that opposites exist complementarily, despite being contrasting forces. This duality can be present in a composition either mildly or forcefully. No contrast is hardly interesting but having too much can also end in chaos. A *yin* and *yang* arrangement is contrast that is designed.

organic/artificial

straight/curved

rectangular/round

soft/edgy

organized/accidental

harmony/chaos

positive/negative

thick/thin

The key tool that has to be considered when trying to use the concept of *yin* and *yang* is balance.

Balance is the point where the frame feels neither boring, nor overly chaotic. It represents the sweet spot where two opposing sides of an element of design can exist in harmony within a frame because their placement and quantity matches up with the opposing visual forces to create a pleasing image.

Here are some examples: straights versus curved, big versus small, busy versus quiet, dark versus light, sharp versus soft, high versus low, one versus many, organic versus mechanical, high versus low, and harmony versus chaos.

Within the various compositions, these complementary elements create an energy and the area of greatest contrast creates a center within the frame. The placement of this area of greatest contrast also needs to be chosen with great care. Dead centre of the frame and close to the edges are both areas that should be avoided as much as possible.

The Bauhaus School of Design was famous for its focus on clarity and minimalism. This exercise from their arts program serves as a great primer to develop graphic sensibility. Learning to think in these abstract terms will do more for your compositions over time than just learning to draw better.

Cut out some small shapes of rectangles and squares in two different colours and try to make different organizations with them on a white sheet of paper. If you prefer, you can replicate a version of this in Photoshop with different layers to achieve the same effect.

Try moving the blocks around to achieve a pleasing arrangement. You will quickly find this is not as easy as it sounds. Notice the negative space. Notice where your eye is going. Notice if the frame feels visually balanced. More than anything else, your goal is to sharpen your awareness of compositional forces at play.

Using these basic elements, try making compositions with specific adjectives in mind. How can you arrange the pieces to create a feeling of unease and tension? How can you arrange the pieces to create a feeling of calm? What other kinds of emotional impact can you squeeze out of these squares and circles?

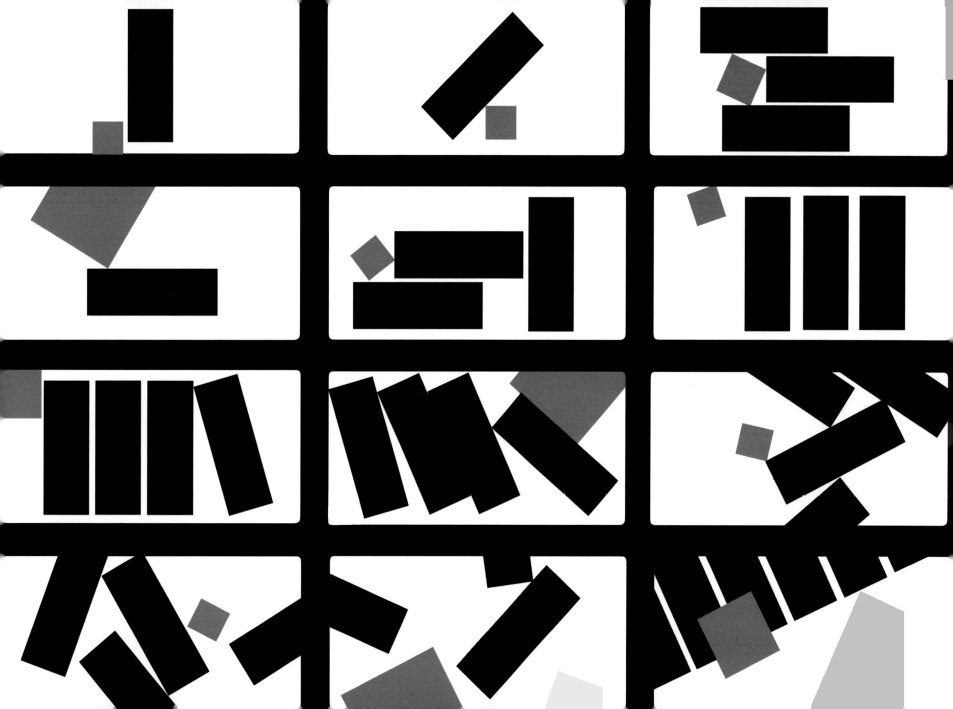

Starting the process in graphic terms will force you to think about your compositions in the right way. Once you gain some confidence organizing abstract elements, you can start to apply this in narrative scenarios.

Replace your simple blocks with more representational elements such as in these examples on the right. You will find that if blocks organized a particular way feel imbalanced, cars organized the same way feel even more so. If a small shape being dwarfed by a much larger shape feels imposing with rectangles and squares, this effect will be magnified when the small shape becomes a character and the larger shape a set of cliffs.

When trying to come up with your next composition, ask yourself: 'What is the simplest graphic statement I can make here?' Once you identify this, remember that the frame gets a certain energy from this underlying arrangement of elements, regardless of the subject matter you put on top. As you add information and detail to refine the frame, make sure you don't lose that underlying graphic statement. Look at your finished frame and ask if a designer from the Bauhaus School of Design would approve.

## Playing with cut and tilted shapes to find the right interaction...

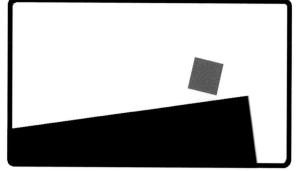
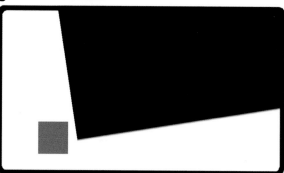

## ...and translated into 'real life'...

or

different impressions
by changing the shapes
from positive to negative

In a way, learning composition is no different from learning how to ride a bicycle. At first it feels like an overwhelming task to keep track of space division, negative space, balance and so on. Much like when learning to ride, turning your hands, pedalling your legs and maintaining balance feel like separate things. Over time though, your brain puts a lot of these on auto pilot and melds everything into one single activity. All it takes is practice. For compositions, the best way to do this practice is thumbnailing.

When making your own thumbnails, keep in mind that it's not about how clean it is but rather how clear it is. It's more valuable for you to do these quickly in small format and trying several rather than labouring over one for hours. Your goal should be to audition several ideas and design arrangements so you have a good selection to pick from. Try doing as many as possible, as often as possible, both for your own images and as studies from others. There is no single faster way to improve your sense of composition.

On the right you can see several real world examples of how the principles we have been discussing translate into thumbnails for film. Study how each of these uses harmony and contrast to create a focal point and interest while achieving balance.

# THUMBNAILS

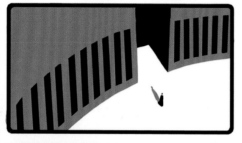

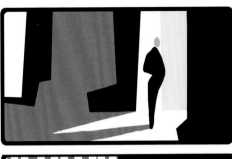

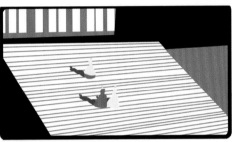

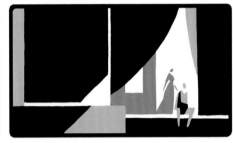

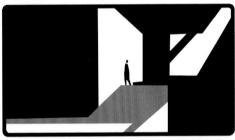

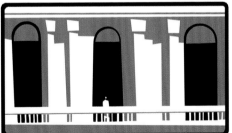

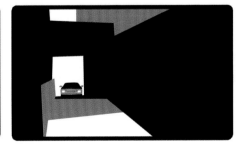

COMPOSING
CHARACTERS

Most movies have a few big set pieces and hero shots that cost a lot of money and get used in all the trailers. While these can be a lot of fun and certainly should be used as opportunities to make some stunning compositions, they represent only a small fraction of the film. A large part of the running time on an actual production usually ends up being compositions with a far less exciting list of ingredients — two or three characters, sitting in a location, talking.

Learning how to compose good compositions with just one, two or three characters on screen is both possible and essential to being a good visual storyteller. This chapter discusses some of the strategies to consider in order to get the most out of character organization in the frame.

# DARK AND LIGHT

Light on dark, and dark on light is a fundamental concept that is extremely effective in making for a clear and readable composition. Always be aware of how the value of your character relates to the value of your background. Unless you deliberately want your character to get lost in the frame, make sure you design and light them to stand out against the background. This can be taken one step further in the realm of color by using warm in front of cool and cool in front of warm.

# PLACEMENT

When dealing with a minimal number of elements in the frame, placement becomes even more important than usual. Make sure your character is balanced in the frame, but not dead center unless you want the frame to feel unnatural. Avoid also the extreme edges where your character gets cropped in strange and distracting ways. As a general rule, it is better to either push something out completely so as not to make a new focal point or pull it in so it is not pulling your eye to the corners. Leaving things floating in a way that is neither here nor there makes for unwanted confusion and is distracting for the viewer. The golden ratio we discussed earlier in the chapter on line can be a useful tool to help position the character in interesting ways.

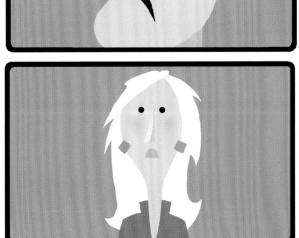

## DEPTH

Adding depth to a composition can go a long way towards adding visual interest. Scaling characters on screen with an awareness to depth can be a simple but powerful technique resulting in incredible imagery. Make conscious choices about the size relationships between the characters in a frame. Can you push the sense of depth between them by making one smaller? Would the shot benefit by a second or third layer of depth? Often this can be as simple as adding rain in the foreground, adding a perspective line in the back or one character in the distance. Does adding a depth cue behind your dominant character help the mood of the scene?

## DOMINANCE

Always aim to have a clear visual hierarchy within elements in the frame. When dealing with characters, too, make sure that in any given shot, one is more important than another or one group is more important than another. This can be done in several ways: make one bigger; make it have more contrast; position it closer to the golden ratio. Your end result should be a frame where there is a clear 'one, two, three' order to characters and focal points within the composition.

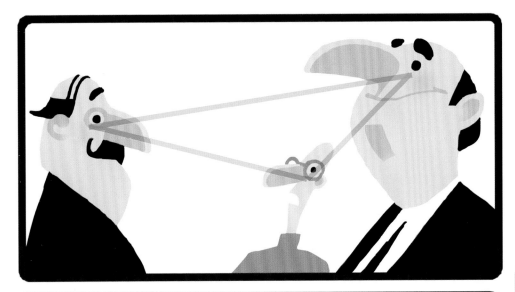

## ANGLES

The relationship between the camera and the character is a core feature that taps into how we relate to the world. Positioning the camera so the viewer is looking down can make a character feel weak. Similarly, looking up at a character usually makes them more imposing and formidable. Be careful not to overdo these or the frame might end up feeling too caricatured and comical.

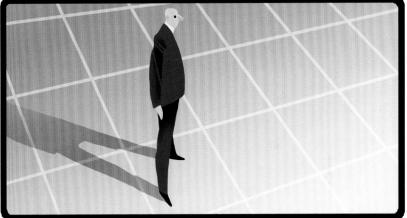

When you have three characters or three focal points in the scene, the viewer's eye will jump from one to the next, creating lines of movement in the image. When designing such a composition, it is useful to think of all the focal points as a connected triangle. Ensuring the shape of the triangle is balanced across the frame and not too symmetrical helps create good compositions.

## TRIANGULATION

# READABILITY

# INTEREST

# *Mood*

Can you tell what is going on?  Does it look interesting? Is the mood right?

Some people thumbnail and build up from that, others collage photos and paint over the top. Some people start with looking at a lot of reference before they pick up a pencil, others like to start with just laying down big shapes and worrying about the specifics later. There are many approaches to creating good compositions, and successful artists for all the different techniques.

As you develop your own artistic ability, you need the freedom to design a process that works for you and takes advantage of your own unique strengths. Experiment with different techniques to find the best fit for you and keep this fundamental truth in mind: Regardless of what route you take towards getting there, the success (or lack thereof) of your composition is ultimately going to boil down to three questions. Can you tell what is going on? Does it look interesting? Is the mood right?

# READABILITY

For a composition to be good, it has to be instantly readable. Most shots in film only stay on screen for three to five seconds. When combined with all the other information being delivered to the audience at the same time such as music, sound and movement, this can easily become too much for someone to process. The solution is to design frames for readability.

Key factors that affect a composition's readability are mostly to do with controlling focal points: the number of them in a frame, how clearly they are defined, how spread out they are, and the amount of time they stay on screen. The following images illustrate some examples of what to aim for and what to avoid when trying to make a frame instantly readable.

Sometimes storytelling and continuity require you to have a lot of elements on screen at the same time. In this case look for opportunities to control the hierarchy of focal points through lighting. The images below show how a spotlight can be used to control the visual information in different parts of the screen.

A common problem in student compositions is the presence of too many focal points. In the image at top, the clouds, rocks and character each create focal points and compete for attention. Reducing the amount of visual information and contrast in the rocks and clouds eliminates these without changing the meaning of the scene.

Use light to centre the attention around your focal points and throw the rest of the scene into relative darkness. Contrast, detail and interesting visual elements should be located in the spotlight and fade off towards the edges as we move away from focal point areas.

Even the face can be treated as a landscape to create a spotlight. Highlighting specific elements is often all you need to get a point across with most of the character covered in darkness. These examples are exaggerated for clarity, but you will find a version of this spotlight in all your favorite films and shows when you start to look for it.

# INTEREST

For a composition to be good, it has to be visually interesting.

It is no small feat for a film to command a viewer's undivided attention for 90 minutes. Every element of the cinematic experience needs to do its part to keep the viewer engaged and stimulated. From a compositional standpoint, this means designing images to be visually interesting.

Making an image visually interesting requires a clear focal point, a healthy balance between harmony and contrast, clear dominance of a few key design elements, and an interesting variety in textures and rhythms.

The following images illustrate some examples of what to aim for and what to avoid when trying to make a frame visually interesting.

One common reason for film compositions not being interesting is a lack of dominance. This can be in the overall theme or in individual design elements. In the image on the left, there is a lack of dominance in values. No visual direction has been committed to, so decisions don't feel cohesive. The result is an image that looks muddy and uninteresting.

Establishing a clear dominance of light on dark or dark on light as shown in the next example makes for a much more compelling image. This allows for a clear definition of what constitutes the negative space in the frame and gives your focal points something to contrast against.

When composing, look for opportunities to establish clear visual dominance. Can you bias the shape, size, value or color of any of the elements to make the dominance more apparent?

Compositions that lack contrast in design elements are not visually interesting. The top composition lacks contrast in shapes, making the image feel stiff and unrealistic. Adding a little bit of variety can go a long way towards making the image more interesting.

In this case, the rhythm and space between the trees lacks variety. Adding more random spacing makes the image feel more natural and interesting. That said, too much variety (as well as too little) can also result in clear dominance. The Goldilocks principle applies!

# MOOD

For a composition to be good, it has to be emotionally appropriate.

The best films are the ones that take you on an emotional journey. They have the capacity to make you feel joy, sadness, anger, fear and more. Our efforts to design frames that are readable and interesting will be for nothing if we do not also design them to be appropriate to the feeling we want to evoke in the audience.

The important questions to ask yourself while designing emotionally appropriate compositions are: Are the individual elements (lines, shapes, colors, etc.) doing their best to express the mood? Are they all expressing the same type of mood or are they contradicting each other? Is there one dominant mood in the image? Is this the right mood for the shot?

The following images illustrate some examples of what to aim for and what to avoid when trying to make a frame emotionally appropriate.

It is essential that compositions are mood appropriate to what they are trying to say. The top composition is too high key, neutral and flat for the dramatic nature of the content. Tilting the camera and changing the lighting makes for more contrast in the image which fits better with the mood.

Here we see the opposite. If this is a moment where the couple is meant to be enjoying a shared moment with romantic music over it, the first image, even though interesting in a different way, is completely wrong. Always pick design elements that work with the mood of the scene.

Creating atmosphere usually involves the principle of less is more. You need to slow the pace and reduce the amount of information requiring audience attention, so viewers have room to take in the moment and focus on feeling.

Often the most evocative compositions, when analyzed, are just two or three simple shapes. Here are examples of readable, interesting, evocative and balanced compositions made with just a few well designed and well placed elements.

Remember, good compositions are not about some great virtuosity in technical drawing ability. It's the art of arranging a few simple things in a masterful way.

# CONCLUSION

Over the last few pages, we have talked about several concepts to keep in mind when creating a composition. We talked about the importance of starting simple. We talked about being mindful of positive and negative space. We talked about *yin* and *yang*, balance and harmony. We talked about how to compose for characters, and how to translate graphic ideas into more representational thumbnails. We also talked about how the holy triad of readability, interest and mood forms the bedrock of all good film composition.

Hopefully all that has given you some new ideas and ways of thinking about your images. Maybe it has even helped you develop some confidence that now you understand composition. And that's great. But the truth is, even if you have understood and applied all this, you are only just getting started.

Mastering the difficult art of composition is a lifelong pursuit. It will take patience and it will take practice. You might certainly be on the right track by reading a chapter on creating interest in composition, but that road continues on for a long way. As you do thousands of compositions you will find your capacity to understand these is built in layers. Over time, your perception of even the simplest words like balance and contrast will deepen to new levels of understanding, perhaps eventually even branching off into your own unique ways of defining and approaching them.

Depending on the path you find yourself using your new set of skills, you will have to add additional perspectives to your knowledge base. Your use of composition may heavily incorporate editing and the vast and wonderful world of continuity based composing. Or perhaps you will venture more towards concept art illustration and your ability to define a location and set the mood will need further development. Perhaps you will find yourself having to forge new paths in combining your understanding of compositions with 3D technology or virtual and augmented reality. Regardless of which path you take, a deep understanding of the fundamentals of composition will serve as a solid foundation to build on.

So keep at it!

Do film studies as often as you can. Develop a shorthand to thumbnail so you can work through several compositional ideas quickly. Revisit this book from time to time and read other books on photography, art, art history, architecture and graphic design. Look at the world from your compositional lens all the time. Buy a camera and also look at the world through an actual lens! Develop systems to make sure you are analyzing your and other people's compositions with the mind of an editor.

If, from now on, whenever you are watching a movie, reading a book or just looking at a poster while waiting for the subway and your thoughts when you see a good (or a bad) composition are ... 'What's working and why? What could be better and how?', this book will have been a success.

This book is the product of a dialogue.

A dialogue between a master and his apprentice that started one evening in Hans's study in Manila and over the course of the next seven and a half years, gradually evolved into what you are holding in your hands.

Like a dialogue, its development has been organic. At the time we started, we had no idea how this would evolve or how long it would take. Over the time we worked on this book, life changed a great deal for both of us.

Hans moved to Singapore to teach, I moved to Canada to start a new job and as other requirements of life sometimes took precedence, this project had to be put on the back burner.

When we would pick up where we left off, things would have to be updated. Time between writing and painting had passed and we would notice a chapter looked or sounded different from older ones we had done. Likely this was because our own outlooks and skills were evolving as well.

Eventually we abandoned our individual ideas of perfection and developed a more organic approach so we were not constantly redoing the entire thing all the time. We hope we still managed to do justice to that parts we felt were most important.

Over the course of these years, Hans and I have gotten to be friends. Concepts you see outlined in these pages were often discussed while drinking beer on a beach in Singapore or sipping tea in an old palace in India. We have visited and gotten to know each other's homes and families and have had conversations about chapters from several cities in the world across many time zones and over countless (constantly failing) Skype calls while also discussing life in general. I believe that ultimately the book was completed because of this friendship.

Hans is a true master of his craft. One of the few of his caliber in our time. It has been the privilege of a lifetime for me to have learnt from and worked with him. We very much hope you have enjoyed reading *Vision: Color and Composition for Film*. We hope you have learnt from it. And we hope that it provokes some interesting dialogues in your own life.

Perhaps, some day, you will write a book about it.

– Sanatan Suryavanshi